T0351379

IMAGINARY BONNETS
WITH REAL BEES IN THEM

Imaginary Bonnets
with Real Bees in Them

Paula Meehan

A collaboration between

THE IRELAND CHAIR OF POETRY

and

UNIVERSITY COLLEGE DUBLIN PRESS
Preas Choláiste Ollscoile Bhaile Átha Cliath

2016

First published 2016
UNIVERSITY COLLEGE DUBLIN PRESS
UCD Humanities Institute
Belfield
Dublin 4
www.ucdpress.ie

ISBN 978-1-906359-91-1
ISSN 2009-8065 The Poet's Chair series

CIP data available from the British Library.

The right of Paula Meehan to be identified as the
author of this work has been asserted by her.

Typeset in Adobe Kepler
Text design and setting by Lyn Davies Design
Printed in England on acid-free paper
by CPI Antony Rowe, Chippenham, Wiltshire

Contents

FOREWORD

In his foreword to Michael D. Higgins's *New and Selected Poems*, Mark Patrick Hederman OSB said: 'Poetry in the broadest sense is probably our only way forward in destitute times.' And he said that 'art alone can provide the weak, yet indispensable, instrument' for this task. These words were written five summers ago – summers with the length of long winters, perhaps, as the community struggled to emerge from the economic depths. But they have continuing resonance for these and for all times.

The arts are not a fair weather friend, a decorative ribbon on the box of life, to be supported when times are good, but to be set aside or left unattended when economic times are tough. It is precisely because of the universal truth that everybody has a relationship with the arts, because of the intimacy of our individual engagement with them, their potential for personal development and their role in creating a sense of community and shared identity that the arts are a vital element in personal and public life at all times, in all weathers.

These lectures are being published while the 2016 commemorative programme continues around the country. The recognition of the role of the arts in the life and sensibility of Ireland and their reflection in the series of national events is an important affirmation of public policy and a statement of commitment that, it is hoped, will be a foundation on which future cultural policy and practice will be built. One of the challenges of public leadership is to bring the community to unfamiliar destinations. Ensuring that the arts, in all their variety, will be as intrinsic an element as any other in public policy priorities will be a continuing test of that leadership.

Poetry, though created alone, is a profoundly communal engagement. It is a gift from the poet to the community, offering new insights into our lives and our world. I recall hearing John McGahern say, in a delightful interview on BBC Radio 3, 'How do I know what I think until I can see what I say?' Knowing what poets say helps us to know fully what we think because it gives a new perspective from which to reflect on our circumstances, a new angle of vision. It enables us to see into the nature of things, to borrow a phrase from Wordsworth.

These lectures and the energetic and selfless engagement that Paula Meehan has brought to her term as holder of the Ireland Chair of Poetry are a living out of the commitment to poetry's place in the public realm that was intrinsic to the establishment of the Chair of Poetry and to the life's work of Seamus Heaney, to mark whose achievement it was created. The celebration of poetic excellence and of poetry itself is central but the bringing of that to the people, through the public lectures, through the residencies in the participating universities and through the other forms of engagement, is the defining characteristic of the endeavour.

For the first time, the series of lectures is being published as the Professor's term comes to an end, reflecting the desirable change in approach that the Trustees have now introduced. For the future, the lectures of every holder of the Chair will be available as single volumes in this UCD Press series at three-yearly intervals. The Trustees have also decided to republish the lectures of the first three holders of the Chair, with their immediate consent and the gracious co-operation of Lilliput Press, the publisher of their collective lectures in the original volume, to ensure that the series of single volume publications will be complete.

Those who conceived this wonderful idea, those who brought it to fruition, the Trustees whose dedication to its success is of a high order, the three Universities, Queen's, Trinity and UCD, and the two Arts

Councils whose support is essential and committed, all deserve great thanks and I am happy to record it here.

And, as ever, we remember him whose life and work was the *fons et origo* of the foundation of the Ireland Chair of Poetry.

BOB COLLINS
Chair of the Board of Trustees, Ireland Chair of Poetry
May 2016

When They Come Alive

C. P. Cavafy

Try to preserve them, poet,
your visions of love,
however few may stay for you.
Cast them, half hidden, into your verse.
Try to hold on to them, poet,
when they come alive in your mind
at night or in the brightness of noon.

Imaginary Bonnets with Real Bees in Them

Poetry can usefully be considered as a negotiation in words between no-mind and mind, between that place where attention is at rest in the void, open to inspiration from otherwhere, and that human place in conscious, directed attention where the rigour of craft finds its natural home.

Here, then, are nine short meditations on poetry – on the obsessive, on craft and inspiration, on the apparently wayward but always mysteriously purposeful flight of bees in my bonnet.

I

The first time I hear the expression 'You have a bee in your bonnet' I'm in Miss Shannon's fifth class in primary school, the Central Model Girls' School, Gardiner Street. I'm in trouble. Again. Usually I'm in trouble for something I've said. This time it's for something I've written. A poem, when I'd been told specifically to write a composition about Milk.

I'm in deep mourning at the time for my dog Prince. Prince got run over by a bus the week before. I wrote an elegy. I didn't have that word then. *Elegy*. Poor dog. Poor dead dog. Miss Shannon thought I was up to something.

'If I wanted a poem, I'd have asked for a poem.'

'But ... '

'But nothing. I'll hear no excuses. And I'll have those three pages.'

Compositions are often done last thing on Sunday night in bed but I have Prince's ghost under my side of the bed and I haven't got an essay – so a poem … who would not love a poem? Miss Shannon would surely love a poem, a poem about Prince. A true Prince, a noble hound.

'You've a bee in your bonnet about these compositions. You'll hand three pages up first thing in the morning.'

I knew what a bonnet was. *Little Women. What Katy Did. What Katy Did Next. Good Wives.* Or our drunken neighbour singing. A party piece. At Easter.

In your Easter bonnet, with all the frills upon it …

Google calls up Irving Berlin's lyrics in the blink of an eye now as I write at my desk in the Shomera, a wooden workroom/studio in the back garden. Dusk, winter. The last crop of borage still a blue, blue intensity in the fading light. Borage: also known as starflower, bee balm, bee bush, beloved of bees, its oil used to regulate and calm the female endocrine system. According to Pliny, borage was the famous nepenthe of Homer which when drunk steeped in wine brought absolute forgetfulness. Bacon says that 'it hath an excellent spirit to repress the fuliginous vapour of dusky melancholie.'

All I know for sure is that the bees, the real bees, bumble bees and honey bees alike, absolutely adore it – and their buzz has been my under-song all year long though now with the onset of winter there are fewer and fewer bees making to the fewer and fewer blossoms. Bees, when they discover a new crop coming into flower, return to the hive and dance intricate signals with coded information in their dancing about these promising sources of food – nectar and pollen. They dance out the exact distance of the food source from the hive and its angle to the sun for the other bees to fix a bead on.

[4]

So, back there in the classroom: elegy. I know Miss Shannon's response is not really about the poem or the unwritten composition or my big mouth. I know that now; I know we're all sad in that room of our childhood for our classmate, Clare, is dead of diphtheria and the public health people have been all over us with tests and needles. Diphtheria! A new word full of menace.

Gentle Clare, with her raven black hair and her blue, blue eyes, as blue as the borage I grow in memory of all my lost ones, my bees in my bonnet. The empty space where she once sat beside me.

II

The American poet, Marianne Moore, is of Irish extraction: her great great grandfather ran away to sea from Merrion Square – at least this is the story that came down in the family and that she liked to put about. 'Poetry', one of her most famous poems, constitutes a flamboyant, some would say drastic, exercise in revision. An *ars poetica* – irreverent, charming, ludic, prematurely postmodern, first published in 1924.

Here's how it opens:

> I, too, dislike it: there are things that are important beyond all this fiddle.
>   Reading it, however, with a perfect contempt for it, one discovers in
>   it, after all, a place for the genuine.
>   Hands that can grasp, eyes
>   that can dilate, hair that can rise
>   if it must, these things are important not because a
>
> high-sounding interpretation can be put upon them but because they are
>   useful.

And here's how it finishes:

however: when dragged into prominence by half poets, the result is
                                                                  not poetry,
    nor till the poets among us can be
    'literalists of
    the imagination' — above
        insolence and triviality and can present

    for inspection, 'imaginary gardens with real toads in them,' shall we have
        it. In the meantime, if you demand on the one hand,
        the raw material of poetry in
            all its rawness and
            that which is on the other hand
                genuine, you are interested in poetry.

The full poem is about twice as long as these excerpts. Now here's her revision, published in *The Complete Poems of Marianne Moore* in 1967:

    I, too, dislike it.
        Reading it, however, with a perfect contempt for it, one discovers in
        it, after all, a place for the genuine.

That's it in its entirety. Three lines.

The phrase 'imaginary gardens with real toads in them' was held out to me when I was a student by more than one teacher, to encourage the validation and valuation of images – striking images, quirky images, clear images, mirror images.

Behind it all was the dead hand of Ezra Pound – *direct treatment of the thing*. By the time I began to seriously set myself the task of learning the honest trade of poetry, the precepts of the imagist manifesto, published in 1916, were deeply embedded in poetry culture. William Carlos Williams's 'No ideas but in things' was used to hammer the message home. I heard the phrase 'show me, don't tell me' so often I *had* to distrust it – why, after all, should an abstract noun be an abomination? What about the music? The tune of the poem? The dance of the poem?

While I could see the use of 'imaginary gardens with real toads in them' as a strategy for building a poem full of the quiddity of the world, the thinginess of creation, I was suspicious of any definite statements about Poetry with a capital P, as wary as I was about grand statements about Politics with a capital P. As soon as a rule or a tendency was proposed, my inner transgressor would, invariably, pipe up.

Marianne Moore has a lovely response to a questionnaire in *Harper's Magazine* (November of 1964) which turns the 'imaginary gardens with real toads in them' precept neatly on its head.

The question was: 'What other pets ... have you? Was there a crow there? Haven't I read that you have a crow?' Moore answered:

> ... when *Harper's Bazaar* asked me for a fantasy I thought I might have one (a crow) adopt me, sleep in the Park or wherever it goes at night, come to see me, wait on me if I wanted my pocket dictionary or an eraser or handkerchief. I wrote that piece, had the crow go to market with me, to the drugstore.

So completely does she make the crow come alive that a neighbour sharing the elevator in the apartment block in Greenwich Village wanted to know '... *where* is that crow of yours?'

She gives us her imaginary New York with the real crow in it, obversely written as the real New York with the imaginary crow in it.

Gardens and toads, cities and crows. Bonnets and bees.

[7]

III

Sister Philippa says I have a bee in my bonnet. I am in her office and I am in deep trouble. The official reason for my impending expulsion from Saint Michael's Holy Faith Secondary School in Finglas is that, with my friends Mary Leader and Marian McDonnell, I have organised a protest march against … well? What? Nuns? The class system? The state of the world? The war with the nuns and their henchgirls had been ongoing since my first day in the place.

'Hands up, who says the family rosary?' Sister Christopher, another nun, that first day. And I didn't put my hand up. We didn't do the rosary at home. She had the rest of the class down on their knees to say a prayer for me and my family. That drew snorts of laughter when I reported it at home; it also taught me the danger of truth telling.

It was all downhill from there. In any case, the interesting stuff was happening outside the school and if I wasn't writing poems I was writing songs and my masters were the young Sandy Denny, Richard Thompson, Joni Mitchell, John Mayall, John Lennon, Bob Dylan, Leonard Cohen, Van our own Man. I'd already been threatened with expulsion when my notebook was confiscated and they found 'vile filth' in it. Said 'vile filth' being my innocent hormone-driven daydreams featuring swords and beasts and wolves, beings of light and creatures of darkness: 'imaginary other dimensions with real teenagers in them.' With friends like John Borrowman of the curly locks and scarlet-lined cloak, lending me the poems of Rimbaud and his own song lyrics, the first poet of my own generation that I met. ('Dracula himself' as my father called him.)

Being thrown out of school was the best thing that could have happened to me.

Not that the frightened child who stood before Sister Philippa thought so. Not after the ritual humiliation of being brought into every single classroom and made apologise for bringing the whole school into disrepute.

Sister Philippa, back in her office, informed me that I had a bee in my bonnet. I felt my mouth opening. There would be no coming back from it, once said. My abject, grovelling, snivelling self that had been frog-marched through the school, that could have, by just a small increase in contrition, redeemed herself, could even have had an outside chance of avoiding the expulsion, was once again subverted by the inner transgressor who shook off her abjection, shook off her snivelling and said:

'Better bees in my bonnet than bats in my belfry.'

Amazing myself. Sealing my fate.

I was sent to my grandparents' house in Marino to escape the bad influences of Finglas. And there in my grandfather's cabinet I found my old friend, a companion to my woes. Emily Dickinson. *The Selected Poems*. The Modern Library Edition, with an introduction by Conrad Aiken. It had always been in the cabinet and it had scribbles of mine or one of the cousins from when we were toddlers. It suited my dark adolescent moods perfectly.

I have it still. Miraculously, I've kept hold of it through all the confusions and vicissitudes of a rambling youth. And this is what my fourteen-year-old self had underlined back then:

> I died for beauty, but was scarce
> Adjusted in the tomb,
> When one who died for truth was lain
> In an adjoining room
>
> ['I Died for Beauty, but Was Scarce']

Mary Leader, my best pal in the convent, was expelled with me. Beautiful girl, a painter and musician. Dead at sixteen. Sister Philippa, at the funeral, couldn't look us in the eye.

John Borrowman, dead at forty-six in Copenhagen.

> Across the evening sky all the birds are leaving
> But how can they know it's time for them to go?
> Before the winter fire, I will still be dreaming
> I have no thought of time.
>
> ['Who Knows Where the Time Goes?']

After John's funeral I sang it through, sang it to the empty sky, and I added my own lines:

'Imaginary skies with real migrant birds in them.'
'Imaginary pasts with real dead friends in them.'

IV

There is a body of Brehon Law in relation to bees, the *Bechbretha*, written down in the seventh century. *Bechbretha* is translated into English as *Bee Judgements* (available in an edition edited by Thomas Charles-Edwards and Fergus Kelly from the Dublin Institute for Advanced Studies). The laws remind us we had ancestors who knew the need to articulate, to be precise in language, in order to be fair to the bees and to the humans who had need of them. The laws remind us now how crucial, how valuable were the honey and wax, precious commodities, all sweetness and light, the marvellous gifts of the bees to our ancestors, and to us.

When I read the *Bechbretha*, I feel I am connecting directly to the aboriginal mind of the ancestors. The ancestors who understood both human community and what I will call, and relish calling, 'bee mind'. How many generations of observing and understanding human nature, and bee nature, did it take for the following to enter consciousness, be assimilated and then expressed:

The man from whom bees escape and who ventures testimony that the swarm enters the land of his neighbour at swarming times: they divide in half between them the produce of that swarm, [i.e.] all produce for three years; but the source of their procreation [i.e. the bees themselves] belongs to the holding in which it [the swarm] settles.

Or this:

The man who finds a stray swarm of bees on a lawful green [the extent of a lawful green in Irish law is as far as the sound of a bell carries, or the crowing of a cock reaches]: it gives a claim to one quarter of its produce for a year to the man who finds it: the other three quarters [go] to the [owner of] the green where it is found.

And this lovely compassionate judgement which gives immunity to the bees in the event they attack:

Among the complete immunities in bee-judgements according to Irish law is the man on whom they have rushed when robbing them, moving them, seizing them [or] looking at them over their hives at the time they are swarming.

These ancestral Irish black bees are buzzing about my bonnet for sure. Especially given that their contemporary descendants are in such danger from the institutionalised mind of the corporations.

Neonicotinoid pesticides, in my view, should properly be termed bio-cides. Neonicotinoids are manufactured and peddled by corporations that are so powerful they can override the sovereignty of states. My own science is often wonky but I know my genetically modified onions and my real bees. The Minister for Agriculture of the Republic where I am a citizen recently (2013) abstained on a vote in Europe that sought to impose a two-year moratorium on the use of neonicotinoids. Limited as it was, this was 'imaginative legislation, perhaps with real breath in it'. And our Minister sat on his hands.

Once, in a cave near Tarbes in the south-west of France, I put my hand in the outline of an ancestor's hand. It is believed to be a woman's hand as, indeed, are many of the hand stencils made by Palaeolithic peoples across the world. The print I'm referring to was made by taking red ochre, possibly in the mouth or in a tube, and spraying it around the hand held against the cave walls. The hand that made it and/or modelled for it is believed to be twenty-seven-thousand years old. That day I put my hand in the hand of the ancient one I felt some deep shift of compassion within me and a kind of wiry tenacious joy take hold of my spirit. I felt it on my pulses, I felt in my hammering heart, and in my deep breathing after, to calm my hammering heart.

I think now of some lines from the 'Third Meditation' by Theodore Roethke, son of horticulturalists, whelped in a greenhouse:

> Was it yesterday I stretched out the thin bones of my innocence?
> O the songs we hide, singing only to ourselves!
> Once I could touch my shadow, and be happy;
> In the white kingdoms, I was light as a seed,
> Drifting with the blossom,
> A pensive petal.
>
> But a time comes when the vague life of the mouth no longer suffices;
> The dead make more impossible demands from their silence;
> The soul stands, lonely in its choice,
> Waiting, itself a slow thing,
> In the changing body.

I don't have to have an actual hand-to-hand with the ancient ones to get a few bees buzzing in my bonnet. I can hardly poke my nose outside the front door without reconsidering this great tradition I'm heir to and wondering where does that leave us poets in our *dinnseanchas*? Last week I stood on Feltrim Hill, beloved of Samuel Beckett, overlooking as it does the coast north of Dublin down towards Portrane and the lunatic asylum there where, in the words of Beckett, 'the tears of the world are held'. Feltrim Hill, the beautifully named Ridge of the Wolves, will soon be flattened if it continues to be quarried, and a new *dinnseanchas* might call it 'Site where materials were extracted to fuel a great economic disaster' but that is perhaps a digression into 'deconstructed ridges with real extinct wolves on them'.

V

The oldest known bee, according to Professor George Poinar in the journal *Science*, is a one hundred million-year-old specimen found in Myanmar – preserved in amber, the hardened sap of an ancient tree; it is at least (at least!) thirty-five to forty-five million years older than any previously known bee fossil.

I access this information through the world wide web, which I prefer to think of as a kind of hive mind. Outward manifestation of the inner space of all who use it, or abuse it, who make a digital intervention in the virtual zone.

The Myanmar bee is the missing link in our honey bee lineage and finding its image on screen is an encounter I find very moving – I am reading the past, the distant past. As I examine the bee in the amber of a million-year-old forest's sap, I am reminded of a poem of Eavan Boland's, called 'Amber', from the 'Letters to the Dead' section of her 2007 book, *Domestic Violence*:

> It never mattered that there was once a vast grieving:
>
> trees on their hillsides, in their groves weeping—
> a plastic gold dropping
>
> through seasons and centuries to the ground—
> until now.

On this fine September afternoon from which you are absent
I am holding, as if my hand could store it,
an ornament of amber

you once gave me.

Reason says this:
The dead cannot see the living.
The living will never see the dead again.

The clear air we need to find each other in is

gone forever, yet

this resin once
collected seeds, leaves and even small feathers as it fell
and fell

which now in a sunny atmosphere seem alive as
they ever were

as though the past could be present and memory itself
a Baltic honey—

a chafing at the edges of the seen, a showing off of just how much
can be kept safe

inside a flawed translucence.

The article in *Science* prompts me to make a beeline to the dictionaries
and before long I'm back with the Greeks: *meli* their word for honey. As
melos is their word for song. Mellifluous melody I'm hearing from the
word hive. And that's before I probe my Dineen, which I see I bought in

Derry in November of 1983, exactly thirty years ago. There I find the *cáca milis*, the sweet cake, and *milseán*, the sweet candy of childhood. And it's there in the Indo-European, the true grandmother tongue for anyone speaking Irish or English. Melit or Medu (medu which gives us mead): English, Latin, Ancient Greek, Sanskrit, Iranian, Slavic, Baltic, Celtic, Armenian, Albanian, Hittite.

Feeling fiercely mellivorous of a sudden, mellivorous being a word that the dictionary angel snags my eye on, and feeling a sudden urgent need to feed on honey, the thing itself rather than its signifier, I open the tin of Ikarian honey. The last of the tins I brought home in June, from the island of Ikaria in the eastern Aegean.

There's a bee's wing, from off a distant cousin to the one hundred million-year-old bee in the amber of Myanmar, intact in the spoonful of honey. The taste of Ikaria. The smell of the mountain suddenly, climbing the Atheros (isn't that a great name for a mountain?) on the way to a panigiri, a village festival where we watched dancers dance till dawn their ancient patterns to a traditional music whose origins are ancient too and may be as significant, for all I know, as the bee's dancing is. Who knows what patterns of nourishment the Ikarians signal? Ikaria is the island Dionysus was reputedly born on, and I believe this in the marrow of my bones after six or seven hours with the music.

The people of Ikaria find it hard to say whether the 'Ikariotikos' is a dance or an instrumental piece of music. Music here cannot be separated from dance. In fact, certain musicians refuse to play the instrumental music without the presence of dancers. The old musicians say they take their measure from the dancers: they fix on the best ones and let them lead them all night in the tunes.

And then to walk down the mountain at dawn, as the earth heats up and the tunes die down and the bees start up. To drowse with all the doors and windows open on the edge of the village and yes, for it is indeed, beyond a doubt, a bee-loud glade, to sleep to the tune of the honey bees.

There'll be honey and yoghurt for breakfast, and we'll sit to counting syllables and recreating the intricate, even fancy, footwork of the dancers in the lines we'll call, if we are lucky, if we are blessed, poems.

Carol Ann Duffy hymns the bees in her collection of 2011, a collection called *The Bees*. 'Bees', the first poem in that book, draws a direct line from a poet's nib to the produce of the bees. The page becomes an 'imaginary dance that maps a route to real honey-flowers'.

> Here are my bees,
> brazen, blurs on paper,
> besotted; buzzwords, dancing
> their flawless, airy maps.
>
> Been deep, my poet bees,
> in the parts of flowers,
> in daffodil, thistle, rose, even
> the golden lotus; so glide,
> gilded, glad, golden, thus—
>
> wise— and know of us:
> how your scent pervades
> my shadowed, busy heart,
> and honey is art.

VI

I first came to Ikaria, a bee drawn to a flower meadow, because of a poem, W. H. Auden's, 'Musée des Beaux Arts':

> About suffering they were never wrong,
> The Old Masters: how well they understood

Its human position; how it takes place
While someone else is eating or opening a window or just walking dully along;

– the poem opens. And keeps on opening.

The museum of fine art in question is in Brussels where Auden meditated before the painting *Landscape with the Fall of Icarus* by Pieter Bruegel the Elder (though this is now disputed), painted in 1565 after Ovid's version of the myth. Auden dates his poem December 1938 and, like the sonnets he wrote in the same year, it carries more than a whiff of the coming times, the sulphur of fascism, the stench of the ovens.

The myth tells of the escape from Minoan Crete of Dedalus, the epitome of a Bronze Age craftsman, and his son Ikarus. Dedalus, you will remember, built a contraption for King Minos's wife, Pasiphae, so that Poseidon's white bull could mount her. She carried the Minotaur to term and gave birth to the half bull, half man, who then had to live out his days in the Labyrinth, a maze-like prison below the Royal Palace at Knossos. Kate Newmann, in her 2001 collection, *The Blind Woman in the Blue House*, has a fine poem in the voice of Pasiphae looking back as an old woman on that escapade:

I saw the bull
and I loved that moment.
I loved him, the way he was.
I understood Europa well then.
Beautiful, white
with long eyelashes above
his big eyes,
and soft skin
on his chest, between his legs.
If you had touched.

['Pasiphae Sat, Old and in Black']

Minos, learning that Dedalus has assisted Pasiphae in her transgression, imprisons him and his son in the labyrinthine prison. To escape, Dedalus constructs two sets of wings. The quill feathers are fastened with thread but the smaller feathers are connected by wax, and Dedalus warns Ikarus in these terms as he straps on the wings and sets their course from Crete for Athens: 'My son, be warned! Neither soar too high, lest the sun melt the wax; nor swoop too low, lest the feathers be wetted by the sea.' The boy Ikarus, does he listen to his father? He does not. The boy flies too near the sun in a rapture of flight, the wax melts, the boy plunges to the sea and is drowned. Dedalus retrieves his body and buries him on the island that is named for him, Ikaria. At least that's one version of the myth. And you can also read the myth as emblematic of the lost wax method of metal casting, brought to a fine art in the Minoan Bronze Age.

It is the poem, as I said, based on the painting that is based on the myth, that drew me to the island of Ikaria in the first place. I feel at home there. I believe I am genetically predisposed to live where lemons grow, where the olive grows, in the bee-loud glades and mountains where the bees feed on wild oregano and pine, where the honey is strong and sustaining, where I can meditate on the nature of failure, on our contraptions that plunge to earth, again and again and again, but were worth the lift into the blue rapture of what is, after all, inner space. Whatever the cost. For we use the myths as mirrors, as we use dreams, as we use poems.

An aside: another of the myths in the Dedalian, if I may, cluster of stories had Dedalus using an actual honeycomb to cast a section of hive in pure gold, again read as emblematic of the lost wax method of metal casting. Michael Ayrton the painter, and the goldsmith John Donald, were commissioned in 1968 by Edmund Hillary, a keen beekeeper as well as the man who climbed Everest with Tenzing Norgay who probably called the mountain Chomolungma. Hillary asked them to replicate the legendary golden honeycomb of Dedalus, and well pleased with the result hung the sculpture in his garden in

New Zealand, where his own real bees used it for their hive and for their young, and made real honey there in the cast gold comb.

The Bronze Age bees are buzzing about my head whenever I teach Auden's poem: and at some point in most discussions someone will talk about the failure of poets in the face of politics, the failure of poetry to stop war, to avert fascist dictatorship, to speak up for the oppressed; or, having spoken for the oppressed, to effect any amelioration of their oppression. Someone will always say, 'and didn't Auden also hold that poetry makes nothing happen? In his elegy for Yeats. Didn't he? Didn't he?'

And that usually closes it all down again.

But, maybe we might read that 'nothing' as a positive thing. If poetry makes *nothing* happen, maybe it stops *something* happening, stops time, takes our breath away. Though, strange that taking our breath away, being breathtaking, is associated with achievement, accomplishment. Maybe it's like the negative space in a painting by which what is there is revealed, to be apprehended by human consciousness.

Perhaps like those marginal spaces that tempted our first manuscript poets, with their bee-quick, jewel-like utterances about some fleeting truth of the natural world, sharp darting glimpses out the scriptorium window – 'imaginary kingdoms of God with real blackbirds singing' as it were – which certainly puts a pleasing spin on the margins moving to the centre.

Maybe the truth in poetry is not in the words per se. The individual words have autonomous force, I would say magic power, in terms of their auditory force on the physical body, and shadow power too in the ghost life of the word, the etymology, the discrete history that each word carries with it, etymologies that if we could trace far enough back might be analogous to hearing the buzzing of the one hundred million-year-old bee in amber.

Much of the truth force of a poem inheres in the rhythmic patterns, or lack of them, the breath patternings, the poem's designs on taking our breath away, the organising of the words into rhetorical patterns, periodic phrases, anaphoric utterance that carries us up, up, up and out of the earthbound stricture of the poem, the craft free of gravity, true agent of flight.

Our truth contraptions. That make nothing happen.

VII

Always, there is someone who has gone before.

A poet wrote this, of the island of Ikaria:

> Here, he feels, is peace,
> The world is not after all a shambles

> And, granted there is no God, there are gods at least, at least in Greece,
> And begins to drowse; but his dreams are troubled

This also:

> And there are prisoners really, here in the hills, who would not agree
> To sign for their freedom, whether in doubt of
> Such freedom or having forgotten or never having known what it meant to
> be free.

Louis MacNeice never names Ikaria but those lines are from a poem set there, called 'The Island', published in *Ten Burnt Offerings* in 1951. I like to think of the poem as 'an imaginary island with real political prisoners in it'. The poem, like the rest of the collection, was generally hammered by the critics when it was published.

The island of Ikaria was used as a prison for the communists during the civil war of the nineteen forties. The impoverished islanders had billeted on them the leaders of the workers, the left-wing intelligentsia, and the artists, including Mikis Theodorakis, the Greek O'Riada; this is where he first heard the wild traditional mountain music and the rembetika, the workers' songs of the Athenian ghetto, and integrated these with his classical training to produce a music that would salve the heart of and strengthen the spirit of the Greek people, especially in times of crisis.

There were still prisoners there in August of 1951 when MacNeice arrived on the island.

Exiling troublemakers is nothing new for Athens: Euripides, the great poet-dramatist of classical Athens (480–406 BCE), was also banished to Ikaria, the birthplace of Dionysus, and found in the remnants of orgiastic rituals, in their music and dance, the lineaments of a tradition that he explored in *The Bacchae*. On Ikaria he found, or conjured, maenads – devotees of long-haired Dionysus, agents of trance dance and transcendental union with the god.

I am typing in the wintry light of a November morning. News of Doris Lessing's death earlier today is buzzing around the virtual zone and reaches me here. I read this on my screen, my interface with the hive mind. I am stung. Exactly that.

I would like to tell the bees Lessing is gone, that a great spirit has left our earth. To observe one of the traditional services to the dead: to tell the bees. Do we tell the bees, as the folk practice has it, so they can carry the news to every part of the parish or as far as the bell carries over a green as the *Bechbretha* delineates human settlement, within sound of the bell? Or do we tell the bees to say irrevocably to ourselves that, yes, the loved one is dead?

I bless the name of Doris Lessing in gratitude, her *Golden Notebook* my handbook to womanhood and the inner city of my body. I've called up on screen whirling dervishes in their Sufic rapture for she frequently made use in her work of the Sufi figure of the hidden master. They make me restless for the out of doors; before the light fades, and in the knowledge that the moon is waxing full, I head for Aideen's grave up on Howth Head.

VIII

Aideen's grave is a dolmen, more usually known nowadays as a portal tomb, at least five thousand years old; there are many folk beliefs and legends clustered about it. Sir Samuel Ferguson's lay, *The Cromlech on Howth*, published in London in 1886, has shaped the folklore since then, challenging our usual belief that folklore shapes the literature. In truth, it is always a dance between two partners. Aideen was the wife of Oscar, son of Oisín, grandson of Fionn MacCumhaill of the Fianna band of warriors.

The local lore also knows the portal tomb as Fionn MacCumhaill's Quoit, one of many Howth associations with the Fenian Cycle of stories where the Head appears in its Irish name of *Binn Éadair*. Whatever the truth or fancy of it as a burial place for Aideen, even in its collapsed state the tomb is an impressive place, overlooking the sweep of Dublin Bay from the north.

You can enter the chamber and lie on one of the fallen portal stones, feel the immense seventy-five tonne gravity of the quartzite capstone above your body. It focuses the mind wonderfully. It certainly focused mine, when I would lie there as a young woman. You must certainly not entertain any imaginings of what might happen should the earth move or should there be a ground tremor. If you can deal with the physical reality, it is a powerful way to connect with the ancestors, to connect with their mysteries.

It seemed to me as a young woman that lying in the tomb was akin to the ancient bardic training of lying with a stone on your belly in the dark, a fine fettling of the soul, an encounter with what William Blake called 'mind forged manacles', one's own deepest fears.

It was at this time in my life too, that I found, cast up on the beach of consciousness, Gary Snyder's *Regarding Wave,* which I hold to this day in the highest regard. There I found the injunctive 'What You Should Know to Be a Poet', a poem I took literally, perhaps after all being one of Marianne Moore's 'literalists of the imagination'. The trick was, as Alan Watts so succinctly put it, to avoid 'climbing up the signpost instead of following the road'.

all you can about animals as persons.
the names of trees and flowers and weeds.
names of stars, and the movements of the planets
                    and the moon.

your own six senses, with a watchful and elegant mind.

at least one kind of traditional magic:
divination, astrology, the *book of changes*, the tarot;

dreams.
the illusory demons and illusory shining gods;

and, the poem goes on:

work, long dry hours of dull work swallowed and accepted
and livd with and finally lovd.   exhaustion,
                    hunger, rest.

the wild freedom of the dance, *extasy*
silent solitary illumination, *enstasy*

real danger.   gambles.   and the edge of death.

And now I am lying in Aideen's grave, thinking of Doris Lessing and *The Golden Notebook*, which I note in one of my own notebooks as 'a d.i.y. manual for cracking up and putting yourself back together again'. It was published in 1962 when I was seven years of age, making my First Holy Communion; it was there for me in those wild Howth days of satsang and satori, lying in wait on my path to detonate with a force that would blast me like some booster rocket into a new space – the other half of the human story, the poems and stories of women – and into a new orbit, 'imaginary spacecraft with real female astronaut in it'.

Dusk, now, and I walk back down the hill. I meet a local woman near the Castle, and the talk turns to the year's honey, the new hives, the practical class in beekeeping over at the Community School. She has no honey to sell this year but will give me a jar for old times' sake.

'Do you remember the plan we had to steal Yeats's tarot deck?' she shouts after me as we part. I carry that line home with me – a little golden sweetener on the night of Doris Lessing's passing, as if that old Sufi herself had arranged the encounter.

IX

She is mis-remembering. I had once pitched a film to my beekeeping friend, in her earlier incarnation as a film producer – the synopsis of which, if I remember rightly, was something like this:

A bunch of teenagers living wild on Howth Head get into magic practices from half-baked notions of druidic lore. They dream up a transition year documentary film project on the poet W. B. Yeats, focusing on the years when he lived in Howth, when he himself was a teenager.

They read his *Autobiographies* and discover on Howth Head the cave he used to sleep in, his ear to the ground so that he could hear the heartbeat of the great mother. They read of how he fell in love with a red-haired girl, a distant cousin, Laura Armstrong, the daughter of an army sergeant. Of how he took the window out of his attic room so he could sleep with the wind washing through.

With the support of their gullible English and art teachers, they go to the National Library in Dublin and, under the guise of interviewing the woman who curated the Yeats exhibition there, conspire to get their hands on Yeats's actual tarot deck. From then on strange things happen in their circle. Not supernatural things but ordinary magical things, black and white: falling in love, betrayal of friendship, gang loyalty, music and drugs and families falling apart – real magic in their actual lives. And all around them, shape-shifting between real and imagined, the beautiful Howth peninsula.

We never did get the production money together.

Yeats used the tarot, astrology, automatic writing, believed in these practices, not a million miles from Gary Snyder's imperatives in 'What You Should Know to Be a Poet' if you remember –

> your own six senses, with a watchful and elegant mind.

> at least one kind of traditional magic:
> divination, astrology, the *book of changes*, the tarot;

Yeats the dreamer is the one I love most. I prefer him to the man of action, the theatre manager, the shaper and shifter. He ends his *Autobiographies* (note the plural), with a meditation on the Nobel Prize for Literature which he was awarded in 1923 and appends this note:

> I was in my Galway house during the first months of civil war, the railway bridges blown up and the roads blocked with stones and trees. For the first week there was no newspapers, no reliable news, we did not know who had won nor who had lost, and even after newspapers came, one never knew what was happening on the other side of the hill or of the line of trees ... Men must have lived so through many tumultuous centuries. One felt an overmastering desire not to grow unhappy or embittered, not to lose all sense of the beauty of nature. A stare (our west of Ireland name for a starling) had built in a hole beside my window and I made these verses out of the feeling of the moment –

> The bees build in the crevices
> Of loosening masonry, and there

The mother birds bring grubs and flies.
My wall is loosening; honey bees,
Come build in the empty house of the stare.

We are closed in, and the key is turned
On our uncertainty; somewhere
A man is killed, or a house is burned,
Yet no clear fact to be discerned:
Come build in the empty house of the stare.

He goes on:

> Presently a strange thing happened. I began to smell honey in places where
> honey could not be, at the end of a stone passage or at some windy turn of
> the road, and it always came with certain thoughts.

Sweet Yeats! His instinct, his intuition, his sixth sense, his watchful, elegant mind.

And now I am home again. An email has come in, a beemail, perhaps, from Jim Holland, enclosing an article he wrote for the November issue of *The Irish Beekeeper*. It ends with a beautiful description of the new queen being introduced into the hive:

> ... the bees will rush to welcome her by fanning everywhere, on the floor of
> the hive, on the sides and on the frames; it is a trumpeting and caroling.

And I swear I can smell honey. At my desk, from the books on my desk. Dineen and the *Bechbretha*, Messrs Yeats and Snyder, Ms Moore and Ms Boland and Ms Duffy, the whole room buzzing, all the bees in my bonnet wide awake. The real and the imaginary worlds fitted one into the other in a glorious golden light.

A transcript of a lecture given in Queen's University, Belfast, on 28 November 2014.
For Marian Dobbin

[26]

The Solace of Artemis

> And then I remember turning and seeing the statue of Artemis for the first time; in that second, as I stared at it, the statue was radiating abidance and bounty, fertility and grace, and beauty maybe, even beauty.
>
> Colm Tóibín, *The Testament of Mary*

The Solace of Artemis, the title of this lecture, is also the title of a poem I wrote a few years ago, inspired by research published in 2011, in the journal *Current Biology*. This research, conducted by Bradley and Edwards here at Trinity College Dublin, in conjunction with researchers at Penn State University and at Oxford University, showed that every single polar bear alive today has mitochondrial DNA from a single ancient Irish brown Bear Mother as a result of a union during the last ice age.

They believe the genome was fixed between whatever was there before the polar bear and our own brown mother bear, possibly as early as fifty thousand years ago, at peak ice, but no later than twenty thousand years ago. The Irish brown bear has been extinct on this island for some nine or ten thousand years, not long in geological terms after the retreat of the ice.

This research, when I came across it, set the hare running or the bear dancing. In the face of anxiety about our future, and that of the many creatures with whom we share this amazing creation, their research offered the comfort of the longer view, the prospect that though we live in cataclysmic times, something will survive.

Can we live, though, with the idea that it may not be us?

Here, in any case, is the poem prompted by reading the article in *Current Biology*:

> I read that every polar bear alive has mitochondrial DNA
> from a common mother, an Irish brown bear who once
> roved out across the last ice age, and I am comforted.
> It has been a long hot morning with the children of the machine,
>
> their talk of memory, of buying it, of buying it cheap, but I,
> memory keeper by trade, scan time coded in the golden hive mind
>
> of eternity. I burn my books, I burn my whole archive:
> a blaze that sears, synapses flaring cell to cell where
>
> memory sleeps in the wax hexagonals of my doomed and
> melting comb.
> I see him loping towards me across the vast ice field
> to where I wait in the cave mouth, dreaming my cubs about
> the den,
> my honied ones, smelling of snow and sweet oblivion.
>
> ['The Solace of Artemis']

This lecture, then, will be an elaboration of the poem; it will concern itself with bears, with memory, and with teachers. It will concern itself with my own span of human memory and with other-creaturely memory, it will invoke the ancient Greek goddess Artemis, the Bear Mother, in whose protection I place myself, whose solace I profit from, in whose territory I build my den against the coming storms.

I

Mitochondrial DNA traces descent exclusively through the mothers. We humans can place ourselves in a line back to the female known as mitochondrial Eve, who lived in the Rift Valley of Africa; we carry the coded poem of her breath in our very bones.

There are, in that line of descent, what I might call intermediary mitochondrial mothers.

The mother I imagine myself descended from is the Bear Clan Mother of the eastern Aegean. This is an elective affinity and comes from a tropism towards Greece and the Aegean that was first fostered through classical references in English poetry. When I began to read poetry, one didn't get very far as a reader without coming across Zeus and Poseidon, Dionysus and Athena and their doings. Stylised and denatured though those poems could be, nevertheless they opened a pathway to the true roots of classical mythology, which is nothing if not the *dinnseanchas* of the Bronze Age Greeks, the lore of place and the endured truths of the people who lived in those storied places.

Artemis in the versions of certain ancient writers is daughter of Zeus and the mortal woman Leto, mother also of Apollo, but Zeus-fathered, Leto-mothered Artemis is a later grafting onto a much older and wilder story.

Her name derives from the Greek word for bear, *arktos*, which also gives us our word arctic – meaning, the place where the bears are. The full etymology or historical meaning of her name has been given as *ark-temnis*, bear-sanctuary. From ancient written sources, augmented by evidence from sculpture, mosaic, and painting, we know that prepubescent Athenian girls 'played the bear' for Artemis, serving as attendants for a year at her sanctuary at Brauron in Attica, and partici-pating in a ritual that involved dancing in bearskins. This is probably a memory of, a later development of, pre-classical ceremonials going back to Neolithic great mother rituals. As Robert Graves warns us in his marvellous storybook, *The Greek Myths*, the names of the gods and goddesses change as different tribes move about and graft on their own versions. Better, he says, to look at what sacrifices and prayers are offered to those gods and goddesses.

As well as with Attica and the Aegean, Artemis has strong associations with Arcadia, that inland zone of pine wood, oak forest and grassland in the Peloponnese, home to the Arcadians, hunters, herders and gardeners, famous in ancient times as independent and tough people, believed by some to be the aboriginal inhabitants of Greece.

Artemis was also the protector of children, of all creatures in child-birth, of all creatures giving suck, including human creatures, and of all wild things. She is a resonant figure for today, when so much of our wilderness is under threat, when so many species of wild animal are facing extinction, when even language extinction is accelerating. This, obviously, is especially true of the languages of indigenous people, the very peoples whose myths and legends contain, like ancient insects caught in amber, vestiges of how we once shared the lives of the creatures as hunters and herders. Some estimates say we lose a language, and its survival strategies, every two weeks.

II

I entered Trinity College Dublin, in October of 1972, to pursue a General Studies degree in Classical Civilization, History and English. I had just turned seventeen.

I would be taught there by the great classicist W. B. Stanford. He seemed to me then, in his marvellous crankitude and anecdotage, something from the ancient world himself, though he was only in his early sixties. He would bring us in examples from newspapers of the misuse of the word myth. It really annoyed him to see it used as a homonym for lie, for untruth, for shaggy dog story, for false science. Myth, he would say, shaking the paper, is 'the Truth, the Whole Truth and Nothing but the Truth'. For the first time I began to see the myths as the ancient truths of the ancestors, their poetry.

Stanford was a great man for making connections. I remember him drawing a straight line of descent from the maenads in their Dionysian frenzy to the frenzied teenagers in the grip of Beatlemania whom he'd seen in O'Connell Street, screaming for John, Paul, Ringo and George. That certainly got our attention, lured us into the thickets of *The Bacchae*, Euripides's great play about the coming of Dionysus to Thebes. Stanford made of Dionysus a version of the long-haired rock and roll gods adored by the zeitgeist, subversive wideners of the generation gap, ecstatic singers of the body electric. The play was a warning to its audience of free-born Athenian citizens, that they should integrate the wild, the ecstatic, the irrational, into the ordered orthodoxies of the state, or suffer the consequences. The implications were not lost on us: we could read a contemporary warning into the play – a warning to integrate the intuitive, the instinctive, the sixth sense of our vestigial animal selves, with the rationalities of institutional mind.

Stanford argued for the sovereignty of poetry in an influential book, *The Enemies of Poetry*. Poetry is not sociology, poetry is not history, is not the sum of the lore and logic it contained, interesting though these things might be; poetry is a way of telling the truth about what it is to be human, a product of the human imagination and a sovereign condition unto itself, coded in measures that are close kin to music and dance.

I had my refuge in the Lecky Library where I would hole up for months, while reading my way voraciously through volumes of poetry and science fiction. The myths were real to me as the poems were real to me – as real and compelling as was the twelfth-century Norman Kingdom of Sicily that I was studying, entranced to find standing in sunlit olive groves and vineyards the same blunt stone towers that stand everywhere in Ireland in their skirts of nettle, briar and lank, wet grasses.

The worlds of home and Trinity were colliding. Back in Finglas, on an avenue called after a patriot, mother bear was dying, her face turned to the wall, the small garden that came with our house too late to bring her solace. Father bear was retreating towards what would become a lifelong stoicism. I saw this and named this, I knew that the word was coined from the philosophers who used to gather at the Stoa of Athens, to argue and debate under that columned portico.

And Artemis was also an alabaster girl in a Victorian glass case in a shop window on Francis Street, Artemis in her Roman version – Diana the huntress: her hound, her quiver of arrows, her lithe limbs, moving through an eternal Arcadia, moving also through my mind. Swiftly, fleet of foot, the grey-eyed one.

Was I dreaming or was I waking, in those years when I was casting about for what solace I could take from the world and the word?

III

My paternal grandfather Walter Meehan, known to all as Wattie, taught me to read and write before I went to school. He would give me a page of his newspaper and a soft pencil that made a mark as black as jet, and he'd have me fill in the hole in every letter 'O'. That was the first letter I knew and I was entranced by the patternings I could find, especially where two 'O's came together, as in moon, swoon, spoon, drool, fool, platoon. All the pairs of owl eyes staring up at me from the newspaper's columns. I graduated to 'D's and 'Q's and 'B's and 'P's and 'R's and somewhere in the transition to the letters with no enclosed spaces, the 'W's, and 'N's and 'Y's and 'Z's, I found myself reading. And often reading columns of horse names, my grandfather being a dog and horse racing man. I imagine I was charmed by the names. I imagine this as an early access to the power of the individual words themselves in their business of proper naming.

And in my grandmother Hannah's kitchen I was learning the hearth words, the common-or-garden nouns that spoke of food and home and fire. She called the kitchen *the scullery*. There was *crockery* and *cutlery*, she washed the *delph*.

[34]

'Every word carries its own ghost with it,' wrote the Russian poet, Boris Pasternak. 'To live your life is not as simple as to cross a field,' is a Russian folk saying he co-opted for a poem.

There is solace in childhood memory, and though I call up the warmth and comfort of the grandfather and grandmother bears, I must also acknowledge a traumatic memory. One night, late, for I was allowed stay up very late in the cave, one winter's night in the late fifties, while rocking on a wooden chair I rocked much too far forward and fell hands first into the slacked, red, heart of the coal fire. My grandfather, sitting in an armchair at the side of the fire, shot out his leg and saved me; only my hands were burned. This I think is my earliest definite memory. A hospital and my hands wrapped in bandages.

My parents, like many of their siblings, were away in England, working, and soon I was despatched to join them in London, where I started school in St Elizabeth's in Kingston upon Thames. My memories from there: learning to sing 'God Save Our Gracious Queen', and longing, longing, to be back with grandfather bear and grandmother bear.

Adrienne Rich, the American poet, remembering her early formal training in poetry, that had her make tight poems in received traditional gestures, said that it was like acquiring asbestos gloves so that she might deal later with the white hot material that would be coming through.

I didn't read her remarks about the asbestos gloves until the nineteen eighties. I found myself suddenly and violently remembering that falling into the fire, as if by that accident I had become, in Yeats's phrase, a 'literalist of the imagination' and the world was made oracle and prescience. For the first time I felt again, found the place in memory for, the pain I'd felt as a child. And what had been sublimated or repressed, or at least struck from conscious memory, was again available to me, a memory I might use as needed, a resource for making, dredged up from nostalgia.

Nostalgia. From the Greek *algos*, pain, and *nostos*, return, homecoming, a not so distant relative of the word nest. The pain of return, homecoming. Not for a rosy-hued childhood, a prelapsarian idyll, an Arcadia, but for things as they actually were, the myth of the self, 'the Truth, the Whole Truth and Nothing but the Truth'.

IV

In the wider web of Artemis lore is the story of the nymph Kallisto, a devotee in Artemis's retinue of virgin followers. Zeus desires Kallisto and, disguised as Artemis herself, seduces her. The son resulting from that union was called Arkas. Hera, the jealous wife of Zeus, transformed Kallisto into a bear, and would have wreaked vengeance on her son, had Zeus not hidden him away in remote and wild country known subsequently as Arcadia. Arkas grew up to be a skilled hunter, and one day in the depths of the forest he came across his mother Kallisto in her bear form. She opened her arms to embrace him. He notched an arrow and prepared to shoot. Zeus, however, moved by a sudden pity, transformed them both into constellations: Ursa Major and Ursa Minor, the big and little bears. And in their names is remembered the Latin word for bear – *ursus*. Any Ursulas in the house?

The land that was named for Arkas, Arcadia, is an interesting and contested space. Hesiod, the eighth-century BCE poet, had mapped Arcadia as a kind of earthly paradise, a version of which made its way into English poetry.

I first came across Arcadia in the cast-off Victorian schoolbooks that Miss Shannon kept in the old wooden presses in the classrooms of the Central Model Girls' School in Gardiner Street. The family had moved back to Dublin from London and though I was not back in the den with the grandparent bears I was close enough to spend as much time as I could wangle with them.

Miss Shannon let those of us who were avid readers read our way through the old books. Some of us were even permitted to borrow them. I established a small library in the bedroom I shared with my sisters and once my interest in reading was noticed I was fed books by the aunty and uncle bears.

In retrospect, hindsight being twenty-twenty vision, I can see that the girl children of the tenements and the inner city social housing were being given the vestiges of a Victorian value system, of a piece with our sewing samplers, with run and fell seams, with buttonhole stitches, with turning the heel of a sock for months on fine steel needles. We were also being educated to be faithful Catholics, to make May altars, to worship Our Lady, the Virgin Mother. The version of Mary that I most loved showed her standing on the horned moon crowned with stars – Stella Maris, Star of the Sea. If we but knew it, this image was rooted in yet another pre-patriarchal version of the moon goddess, grey-eyed Artemis herself, the Bear Mother. We were also being prepared, in the run up to 1966, to commemorate the founding event of the Republic, the Easter Rising. Our little girl hearts were bursting with ideas of the heroic; we were ready to die for Ireland.

The family lived near the school in Sean McDermott Street, named for one of the signatories to the Proclamation, as the streets of the poor so often were. Albert Camus asks us to dance 'beyond hopelessness and beyond hope', which is all I can do when faced with what we have made of that document and its promises. And it was to our second floor flat I brought home the relics of Empire, the primers of the Victorian age. It was a corner flat and though the front door of the house was on Sean McDermott Street, its high windows looked out onto Gardiner Street, named for Luke Gardiner, First Viscount Mountjoy. Even then I could sense the ironies gathering around me, as I read my way through those Victorian schoolbooks, a child of the Republic stumbling into the language of the Arcadian sublime.

Said sublime I could find in any case, simply, daily after school as I rambled with my friends through abandoned tenement rooms, seeing what we never knew how to name: what oppressed and delighted us at one and the same time, in the stucco and other fine work of the Italian craftsmen all over the old and mouldering Georgian tenement houses of the north inner city. O nymphs, O dryads!

Though the poems in the old primers were hard, and I might sometimes glaze over at litanies of gods and goddesses, there was a pulse beyond or even between the words there, a music, an enchantment, a sense in the pit of the stomach of being in the presence of power.

There was an access to a virtual world where I intuited I could have power and agency, a power only limited by my capacity to understand what the words meant, and also how they sounded and resounded their meaning. I was delighting also in the visual shape of lines, the patternings of verses on the white page, as much as I was delighted by what all of this could make happen in my mind.

I've wandered a bit from the aboriginal homeland of Arcadia, where bears and wolves roamed virgin forest under the eye of Artemis, and our young hunter Arkas is about to be embraced by his mother Kallisto the bear – but isn't this how it is for us as readers, the world doubled with itself, *topos* and *logos* inextricably intertwined?

By the time of Blind John Milton's masque *Arcades*, presented as an aristocratic entertainment on 4 May 1633, the wild and the wilderness had been subsumed into the English pastoral, made effete, sublimated, denatured, albeit framed in beautiful cadences.

Even as I became aware that the dead hand of that tradition was the hand that fed me, I knew it was a hand I would ultimately bite. I was learning to decode these clues that led to a vision of the natural world, of aboriginal dreamtime, as I found it pied, coded and scrambled in this pastoral poetry – degenerated in the transmission, certainly, but present nevertheless in the hints and nuances of an older, wilder, relationship with an animal self that might be truly at home in creation, free of dualism.

V

The first time I set foot in the New World, 9 September 1981, I landed into a flat on 4th Street, on the Lower East Side. There in a magazine, or a journal or an anthology or maybe even in the collection in which it originally appeared, *Body Rags* (1967), I found Galway Kinnell's poem 'The Bear'.

I was staying in New York a few days before heading up to the north-west, to Washington State, to be a teaching assistant in the Master of Fine Arts writing programme at Eastern Washington University. Kinnell's poem snagged my attention – there would be woods up there in the far north-west, woods with bears in them.

As much a poem about his human hunter and about the mind of the poet tracking them both, as a poem about a bear then, 'The Bear' opens thus:

> In late winter
> I sometimes glimpse bits of steam
> coming up from
> some fault in the old snow
> and bend close and see it is lung-colored
> and put down my nose
> and know
> the chilly, enduring odor of bear.
>
> I take a wolf's rib and whittle
> it sharp at both ends
> and coil it up
> and freeze it in blubber and place it out
> on the fairway of the bears.

When the bear has taken the bait and the wolf's rib bone begins to uncoil within him and he begins to bleed, the hunter follows the blood-trail, begins to eat the blood-soaked faeces of the animal. A curious transformation is underway. When the hunter comes on the bear's carcass on the seventh day he tells us:

> I hack
> a ravine in his thigh, and eat and drink,
> and tear him down his whole length
> and open him and climb in
> and close him up after me, against the wind,
> and sleep.

> 5
> And dream
> of lumbering flatfooted
> over the tundra,
> stabbed twice from within,
> splattering a trail behind me,

And then the poet, the hunter, having dreamt himself a bear, awakes from his bear *aisling*, he thinks, and the poem ends with a vision of a dam-bear, a she-bear, in a ravine under old snow; she is giving birth, or cleaning up a cub, or possibly even cleaning with her tongue the fallen body of the male bear, for all these readings are possible – 'licking/ lumps of smeared fur/and drizzly eyes into shapes/with her tongue.' The poet is left to wonder:

> what, anyway,
> was that sticky infusion, that rank flavor of blood, that poetry,
> by which I lived?

A sustained meditation then, also, on nourishment, poetic nourishment, which involves a sacrifice and a transubstantiation.

[40]

It was the pre-Christian, specifically the pre-colonisation, worldview I was after, when I headed north-west.

One of the students, a Vietnam veteran, was a gifted hunter, he supplemented our meagre larders with salmon and deer; himself and his wife would take us into the forest, camping and trekking. They could decipher from the spoor of wild animals just what was eating what, and when, and, always conscious of our fragile place in the food chain, they minded us kindly on these trips.

It was with this couple one autumn morning that I saw my first bears outside of zoos. Grizzlies (*ursus arctos horribilis*). Somewhere in the Northern Cascades, in the borderlands between Washington State and British Colombia, not even certain which side of the border we were on, we had just forded a creek bed when we spotted a she-bear and two young bears near her, aged about a year and a half, our friends thought. The bears were feeding on berries. Raking the berries into their mouths with astonishing grace for such huge beings. In the bright autumn sunshine, that had not yet banished the icy cool of morning. Our friends came over very serious indeed and we moved slowly, carefully and very quietly back across the creek and away.

In Washington State I was seeing something of our own island's aboriginal past. The Fianna warriors were deer and salmon people; Oisín was hunting deer with his friends at the edge of Loch Léin down in Kerry when he saw Niamh and began his journey to Tír na nÓg. And here in the indigenous population were deer and salmon people who had lived an essentially Bronze Age existence by European measurements up until a scant one hundred years before. I felt I was putting my fingers on an important pulse. I would never hear our own old stories the same way again.

I printed Galway Kinnell's poem out some weeks ago in preparation for this lecture and it was on my desk when news came through that he had died at the age of eighty-seven.

I spoke the poem out. As I finished saying the lines to myself, I closed my eyes: I have an intense memory of tracking my father one morning in the snow, stepping into each crisp imprint that he made along the North Wall dockside where he's come to see about some casual work in a warehouse over the Christmas. I am shadowing my father through the radiant light of winter. No work to be had. It is the end of childhood and something in me knows that. And something in me knows that I will sing this journey out into the cold November air, that I will translate his taciturnity into song. I see my father now as a wounded bear. Once when I asked him to make a recording of his memories of his life, he said 'I don't do the past.'

> and the ordinary, wretched odor of bear,
>
> blows across
> my sore, lolled tongue a song
> or screech, until I think I must rise up
> and dance.

If Galway Kinnell, so to speak, greeted me on the threshold of the New World, I was already much taken by that generation of poets who had found in Buddhist thought a powerful survival strategy for the oppressions of nineteen fifties America. A luminous figure among these, an ecologist and poet of the north-west, whose poetry was map to both the world outside and the inner world of dream and vision, was Gary Snyder.

Gary came on campus as Distinguished Visiting Poet, a powerful, focused, humorous presence. His first workshop may not even have mentioned the word poetry. It was all about breathing. Yes, I know, breathing is not something one goes to university to learn. It is a natural reflex. But there's breath and there's breath. I found myself standing there in the familiar workshop space, a space I loved, understanding for the first time just how profound a privilege it was to be alive. To be breathed by the universe. To take a breath, to hold it, to let it go. After intense argument and the intellectual rigour of the workshop training, such a sense of solace to bring the poems back home to the body.

— What will we do with fear though, Gary?
— Ah, one breath meditation.

To slow the entire cosmos down to an awareness of this one breath, the simplicity of it.

My craft teacher there in Eastern Washington University was James J. McAuley, the Dublin poet who directed the writing programme, and ran the workshop where we studied our craft, where his students, seven or eight of us over the two year programme, brought our poems week after week into the ferocious light of each other's honest, sometimes brutally honest, critique. Jim was master craftsman himself, deeply learned in the traditions of poet-craft here on the home island, but living and teaching in the States since the nineteen sixties he was immersed in American poetics and radical theories of prosody. New ways of making.

It was a lucky day that I became his student. He had a working knowledge – better, a working *memory* – of Anglophone poetry that stretched right from earliest times to the present moment. With Jim, I learned to face what I call now the karma of the received forms, the inhabitation and re-inhabitation of these forms through historical flux, to take these cast-off shelters from another age and remake them as places to live and breathe in again. A kind of liberation, a kind of solace in form.

Jim encouraged us to situate ourselves in a continuum that encompassed the radical re-estimations of myth and history then sending cataclysmic tremors through the university, a profound change that would see the establishment of women's studies programmes, affirmative action, and a changed relationship to hierarchical ideas around the canon and who makes it, who shakes it. Who decides who is important and why?

When I visit him now, in his retirement here in Dublin, I have no way to meaningfully express my gratitude for the friendship and teaching of those years. We sit in silence. He wonders who I am.

I will let this small poem say thanks:

It's not just that he can't remember
you: he can't recall any of it:
the university, his other
students. I rocked. I reeled. I was knocked
off kilter, as if the child in me
had stepped up to the blackboard and picked
up the chalky duster and wiped her
future lines away, even the bit
where he helps me get sober and clear.

['The Old Professor']

I offer three bows of gratitude to the teacher bears.

VI
Marija Gimbutas, in *The Goddesses and Gods of Old Europe* (1982), tells us this about Artemis:

in her various manifestations – strong and beautiful Virgin, Bear-mother, Life-giver and Life-taker – the Great Goddess existed for at least five thousand years before the appearance of Classical Greek civilization. Village communities worship her to this day in the guise of the Virgin Mary. The concept of the goddess in bear shape was deeply ingrained in mythical thought through the millennia and survives in contemporary Crete as 'Virgin Mary of the Bear'.

Ancient history, the history of pre-literate peoples, may well be sifted through with speculation, but the written record doesn't necessarily make formal history any more reliable. Who gets to tell the story, who survives to tell the tale, obviously tells their side of the story. Who gets to look back is also a question of access and imagination. Memory, private, communal, folk or institutional as it manifests in poetry, in myth, manifests in code, sometimes exceedingly pied and hidden. Ancient memory, often garbled, mysterious, dreamlike, having come through so many mouths to our twenty-first-century ears, is a song of survival. Whatever is held in the myths – like bee wings in amber, like fossilised trees – resonates in the living body, the way a poem might use the human body, in the ritual re-enactment of the breath from which it is made, to re-experience itself.

Over there in the New World, having seen the bear in its own habitat, the bear lore of both the traditional stories of the native peoples and the contemporary poetry of the day seemed to come to me from an unbroken tradition, though sometimes with slightly surreal implications.

Once at a pow-wow by the Spokane River where tribes of the north-west had gathered, each with their ceremonial drum, I watched the dances. The saddest dance was the newest dance: one man on his own danced the dance of the Vietnam veterans. The only man left of those who'd come home to that particular tribe from the war. Danced like a wounded bear.

Let me give you another bear poem, a poem called 'Destruction' by the Californian poet, Joanne Kyger. I love the way the very person of the bear rampages through the hip detritus and ideas of the American countercultural zeitgeist.

First of all do you remember the way a bear goes through
a cabin when nobody is home? He goes through
the front door. I mean he really goes *through* it. Then
he takes the cupboard off the wall and eats a can of lard.

He eats all the apples, limes, dates, bottled decaffeinated
coffee, and 35 pounds of granola. The asparagus soup cans
fall to the floor. Yum! He chomps up Norwegian crackers

stashed for the winter. And the bouillon, salt, pepper,
paprika, garlic, onions, potatoes.

                                         He rips the Green Tara
poster from the wall. Tries the Coleman Mustard. Spills
the ink, tracks in the flour. Goes up stairs and takes
a shit. Rips open the water bed, eats the incense and
drinks the perfume. Knocks over the Japanese tansu
and the Persian miniature of a man on horseback watching
a woman bathing.

                             Knocks Shelter, Whole Earth Catalogue,
Planet Drum, Northern Mists, Truck Tracks, and
Women's Sports into the oozing water bed mess.

                                         He goes
down stairs and out the back wall. He keeps on going
for a long way and finds a good cave to sleep it all off.
Luckily he ate the whole medicine cabinet, including stash
of LSD, Peyote, Psilocybin, Amanita, Benzedrine, Valium
and aspirin.

VII

Because of her manifestation as a moon goddess, and the particular light that is moonlight, Artemis is associated with silver leafed plants, and there is a genus of plants *artemisia*. Everyone has seen fretty silver mugwort; it loves the rough ground of dereliction and is an active coloniser. It is everywhere in the city and the suburbs.

Less common is common wormwood, largely a garden plant here. *Artemisia absinthe*, its botanical name, is a clue to one of its traditional uses. It was the signature ingredient in the hallucinogenic drink beloved of Picasso, Baudelaire, Rimbaud.

[46]

But, as its folk name implies, it is as a wormer, a vermifuge, that it has been used in folk medicine. I grew it in County Leitrim back in the late nineteen eighties. I remarked casually to a neighbour that it was a wormer and told him some of the strange and interesting and often reliable lore I'd gathered from Mrs Grieve's 1931 *The Modern Herbal* and Culpepper's 1653 *Complete Herbal*, two books that let me probe, as it were, the memory of the hedgerows of Leitrim. Many months later, one deep winter night, there came a knock on the door and a very old man. He had about three overcoats on his body and he said he came from over near Sliabh an Iarainn, the iron mountain. He was like something out of a fable. He said: 'I hear you have the cure for the worms.' I cut some of the feathery grey leaves with due warnings that I had no cure but only book learning. I especially warned him not to take any herb himself. I refused his offer of money. He went off. He never came back.

One kind of memory colliding with another.

I'm acutely aware that this story of the man at the door is from a time before we had to deal daily with machine memory, which digitises sound and image. Back in the city again, I found myself, in the early nineties, at a workshop in the Apple Lab in Trinity College that began with the words: 'Sound is memory hungry'. Though it referred directly to machine memory I saw that it could apply to poetry. *Poetry is memory hungry.*

And I thought then of all the poetry we had committed to memory since the girl-children in their bear skins danced for Artemis. I thought that perhaps, in the new media, a new oral poetry was to be unleashed and developed. And I was partly right; but experiencing poetry on the internet, say through You Tube or Vimeo, is only a simulacrum of oral culture, where direct transmission is an important part of what is passed on, the tradition itself made manifest in sound waves, in the patternings of human breath, if you will. In digitised sound the waves are translated into bits, something is lost; what we get is the human voice flattened, denatured.

I revisit my younger self now, in the Lecky Library that disconnected year of my mother's dying, immersed in ancient poetry and also in science fiction. One of the commonest tropes in the science fiction stories I was reading was of a group of humans landing on a far planet where all life, or sapient life at least, is extinct. They find in a cave or a man-made bunker deep underground a machine that holds the memory of some vanished human or human-related species, once top of the food chain, now perished due to misuse of resources, unquestioned indulgence of greed. They had failed, as I fear we are failing, to marry the resource and wisdom of *mythos* with the vaulting ambition and powers of *technos*.

VIII

In the New World I came across many animal bride, animal groom stories, and a central story told by many of the first nations people was *The Woman Who Married a Bear*. Every culture, if you trace back, holds in memory this idea of intercourse, of profound conversation between the humans and animals.

The European animal groom and bride stories got written down very early – the classical writers, the sixteenth-century French writers, the nineteenth-century philologists, the Brothers Grimm. It gets hard to see the lineaments of the original forest tales in the literary ornamentation, especially after the Enlightenment with its emphasis on rationality and the analytic. The Oldenwald, the Old Forest, once written down and rewritten and rewritten, becomes a mere backdrop, instead of integrated system. Even long before Hollywood gets hold of it – an arboretum rather than a forest.

Which is why the versions of indigenous peoples are so valuable. They hold in memory, like bee wings in amber, both original energies of and a template for, should we choose to avail of it, a wise and co-dependent relationship to the wild and to each other in community. It would be delusional to think they might save us as we stand on this brink of global extinction, but the hard won vision may offer a clue to a saner, lighter tread on the earth. Our only hope is a change of mind.

I drew on Native American and other sources when I was asked by the National Theatre to write a 'fairytale' for the 2003 Christmas show at the Peacock for children. I made up an animal groom story, a girl who mates with a wolf. I found it a useful way to speak of the uncontrolled development that was happening in Tiger Ireland at the time, to talk of the extraordinary riches we had been given and the uses we were making, or failing to make, of them.

Once in Prince Edward Island, on the north-eastern seaboard of Canada, to read poetry at a conference:

In the Anglican Church in the capital, Charlottetown, I opened my reading with a poem by a poet of the indigenous Micmac people, Rita Joe. I knew nothing about her but I felt that it was honour due to the people and to the place. I was especially determined to do so, because one of the conference people had sneered at her work. It was the kind of sneer, dismissive of an aging woman writing a poetry of direct witness out of her own experience, that I was well used to hearing and decoding, and resisting, at home in Ireland.

Some Micmac students in the audience were astonished to hear Rita Joe's words resounding in the church with its perfect if ironic acoustic, the church itself a symbol of the coming of Christian and colonist. There was to be a naming ceremony for a new tribal drum that had been recently commissioned, where, incidentally though probably not co-incidentally, the new Keeper of the Drum was a young Micmac called John 'Wolf Boy' Ward. Yes. A Mac an Bháird. Son of the Poet.

I was given a present of a profound and wonderful book: *Stories from the Six Worlds: Micmac Legends.* And in it I found this person, upon whom I based one of the characters in my 'fairytale':

One of them was a boy
He was blind from his birth,
But he frightened his mother by his sight.

He could tell her what was coming,
What was coming from far off.
What was near he could not see.

This little fellow is always in trouble, a nuisance and a danger around
the fire because of his blindness but he can see two mountains over.
Whatever is coming down the trail is their future.

IX

The poem 'The Solace of Artemis' of which this lecture is, as I remarked
at the start, a kind of unpacking, is dedicated to Catriona Crowe, a
remarkable archivist, who works at the National Archives here in
Dublin, who put the 1901 Census and the 1911 Census online, and who
understands the role of archival memory in empowering people. From
her work I have been able to repopulate, literally to re-member, the
house, the street, the strange no-go area at the heart of Dublin, that
was named Monto, the birthplace of grandmother and grandfather
bear – Wattie and Hannah.

I go online into the census records of 1911 when I need to be close to
them. I reach for them through a fog of some doubt; a census relies on
people telling the truth, and this becomes the truth of the written
record on which we rely. I imagine many of the inhabitants of Monto,
the biggest red light district in Europe at the turn in to the twentieth
century, may have had issues with speaking truth to any authority. So I
have to search for the truth through family memory, folk memory and
written memory – a perilous and far from simple operation.

Hannah is six years old in 1911, living in 49 Lower Tyrone Street. We
can see from the 'Darkest Dublin' collection of photographs just what
conditions Hannah was living in with her father Joseph, a thirty-
seven-year- old carter, her thirty-five-year-old mother Annie, and her
five sisters back in 1911. The details I can glean: they are Roman
Catholics, they are all Dublin born, they can all read and write except
for the two youngest girls, Chrisdiania and Annie junior. What an

unusual name, Chrisdiania, and my grandmother's name is spelled
J-o-h-a-n-n-a-g-h. I file these spellings under mystery, for there is no
one left alive to ask.

Wattie is harder to place. There's a Charles Meehan, his father, who
seems to have acquired 85 and 86 Lower Tyrone Street by 1911 from
Lizzie Arnold, who in turn acquired them from Annie Mack, those
models for Joyce's madams in Nighttown, who operated principally
out of these houses. So that's the first written clue that there were once
brothels in the family.

In the 1911 Census I find Wattie there in number 87 Lower Tyrone Street,
at the age of ten, next door to the two bawd houses with his mother,
Anna, the madame, three servants, though that term could mean any-
thing, and two brothers. The return says Anna has nine children, seven
still living, but I can find only three boys enumerated with her.

But Wattie, in 1911, also appears to be living with his father Charles, at a
different address, nearby in a house of men, on Mabbot Street, where his
age is given as six. His parents, without children, live in that same house
in the 1901 Census of a decade earlier. Did Anna, the madame, have nine
children in that decade, while managing a growing business, accumulating
property and notoriety? The closer I come to them the further they recede.
And what am I searching for anyway? Some consolation in a story?

I never heard a word of this history from within the family. Some stories
just don't get told within the family and home truths are often found
way outside the home.

It's Terry Fagan of the North Inner City Folklore Project who comes up
to me one day on Summerhill and says 'I have great material on your
great grandmother, Mrs Meehan.' One version, for the versions are
coming out of the oral, tells me she got religion and left much of her
ill-gotten gains to Frank Duff, the founder of the Legion of Mary who
mounted a crusade on the last of the bawd houses, when it was safe to

go in there, when the garrison had pulled out and the docks were declining, and the new state with its constitution ghost-written by an archbishop was busy consolidating its power.

Hannah and Wattie then: baby bears on Lower Tyrone Street in the new century, lost in the forest that is red light Monto, finding each other. Growing through the century their web of love and devotion, to each other, to their children, to their grandchildren; and never a word about their origins, all the lore and story obscured or lost, just when I so desperately need to hear it.

But, and such is the power of memory, of language, I can reach back there to console the child with the burned hands, to tell her nothing is ever lost that has made its way into poetry. Safe back there in the loving kindness of grandfather bear and grandmother bear, she is learning to write. In the books that Miss Shannon gave her, she is finding her way home to the Bronze Age comforts of ritual and myth; in a creek bed in Washington State she is watching a mother bear teach her cubs; in the Lecky Library she is dreaming the past and the future; in the witness of poets and teachers she is learning the truths and sorrows of the one and only world we will ever know. And she is learning her trade, is *still* learning her trade, even as I write out her story, or part of it anyway, under the wise and loving gaze of the enduring Bear Mother, the still-enduring bringer of solace, grey-eyed Artemis herself.

A transcript of a lecture given in Trinity College Dublin, on 24 November 2015. For Catriona Crowe

Planet Water

I begin this lecture with rain bucketing from the heavens, on its way from the clouds through the underground drainage arteries into the rivers, and then into the sea from where it will lift again into the clouds, a great cycle of being and becoming that both sustains us and, as it happens, gives me the impetus to embark on this wayward odyssey.

For this journey I need the language of water, a tongue that can speak in river vowels, in the glottal stops of rapids, a language turned in the great tides and braided on the shores of the world, the music of floods and calving glaciers, the deep-delved riffs of springs and wells, the melodies of beck and brook and burn, the harmonics of rain and tarn and lake, snow tunes, sleet tunes, ice tunes, ballads wrought of drizzle and mizzle, the wild tattoo of hailstones, standing here in the liminal zone of my present home-place, the low lying estuarial land of Baldoyle where the River Moyne, locally pronounced Mayne, flows into the Irish Sea. A small river, not much to look at, but it drains a huge area of north Dublin and irrigates the eel grass that is the staple winter feeding of our most distinctive visitors, the Brent geese.

Thus began the meditation on source, on resource, on water and the unconscious, that informs this lecture.

I

Last autumn, the radiant autumn of 2015, I stood in a wooden house on the banks of Great Village River, in Nova Scotia. I was in the childhood home of the poet Elizabeth Bishop, in the home of her beloved grandparents, William and Elizabeth Bulmer. Here in 1916 Elizabeth Bishop experienced the profound crisis that would mark her forever, the breakdown and subsequent committal to a psychiatric hospital of her widowed mother, Gertrude.

I stood in sunlight in the pantry off the kitchen. I drank a large glass of water from the well below the house. In Elizabeth's childhood the water would have been pumped up by hand, but I just turned a tap and let it run for a few minutes, then drank deep of the sweet and perfectly clear water.

I wanted to speak her poem 'Sestina' in the very kitchen that was its locus. I might not have done this at all, not wanting to impose myself on the peace and plenitude of the house, but when I got there it seemed the right thing to do. I took heart from seeing on the walls in one of the downstairs rooms poster poems by both Eavan Boland and Seamus Heaney. They seemed to me guardians of the space, and if the soul does select her own society then this was surely an omen that it would be alright to bring another Irish accent into the zone, into this kitchen I felt as a sacred space, a temenos.

The poem named 'Sestina' is just that, a sestina, a shining instance of that most difficult traditional poetic form, and an excellent one to use as an example when teaching the form itself. There are many variations of this pattern inherited from the medieval Occitan troubadours, but Elizabeth Bishop uses the strict rubric.

Bishop's sestina is a masterclass in the artifice that conceals art. If you read it without preamble to a class of writing students they will invariably relate first to the narrative, to the simple kitchen imagery of a child drawing a house, the kettle on the stove, the almanac of rural life with its forecasts and market days and moon cycles. The writing students will be opened emotionally to the abyss of grief conjured by the mesmeric patterning, without necessarily knowing they are being coldly, craftily manipulated.

Here is how it ends:

> But secretly, while the grandmother
> busies herself about the stove,
> the little moons fall down like tears
> from between the pages of the almanac
> into the flower bed the child
> has carefully placed in the front of the house.
>
> *Time to plant tears*, says the almanac.
> The grandmother sings to the marvelous stove
> and the child draws another inscrutable house.

The morning before I fly home from Nova Scotia, I am offered an intriguing visit. The poet Sue Goyette, whose work, though new to me, has already had a profound effect on me, suggests I go and have my tea leaves read. I take this suggestion as an invitation from the universe and turn up on the threshold of a very ordinary looking apartment. I am expecting someone like my maternal grandmother, Mary McCarthy, who was a gifted amateur psychologist and a dinger at the leaves. She used the gift of prophecy, or perhaps it was native shrewdness, to keep her daughters, my mother included, in some kind of line.

I sit at the woman's kitchen table and drink a fragrant jasmine tea. But the leaves are never read; she reads my cards instead. It's not a deck I'm familiar with. It uses animal spirits for what in more traditional tarot decks are called the major arcana. My female energy, The Bear, it seems, is strong and earthed; my male energy, The Peregrine Falcon, is powerful, she tells me, I have vision and focus – though while hunting I have a tendency to fixate on one object, the prey, to such an extent that I might miss other opportunities about me.

It is at this moment that I have an overwhelming sense of wind rushing through my feathers, of a small creature darting to safety as I swoop from above. Suddenly I am sweating and the kitchen is now a sea cave of pulsing light. Her voice has become hypnotic.

This card she tells me, turning it over, is The Querent – myself, the one who comes with a question. I am standing on a horned moon in a tranquil seascape. There is a crab at my right foot and a three-headed dog in a guise of guardianship before me. It is an affirming and beautiful sensation, listening to her slow voice unfolding in the pied and symbolic way a poem might, perspectives on my deepest fears and hopes.

Then she has me sit before a large mirror. She looks beyond me into the depths of the mirror to read my past lives. I feel complete and absolute trust, what she is telling me rings true. When you immerse yourself in the patterning of the world, she says, you merge in the great sea of the unconscious, a kind of universal mother, so that self is transcended and the vessel that contains the ego is dissolved. This can bring a tremendous sense of relief, yes, but the danger is that it gets harder and harder to reconstitute the vessel, to gather a coherent self back into a container. To live the daily life.

I can feel myself soaring, it might be for hours or minutes, I cannot tell, then I am hanging in air a moment, then riding a thermal down and through the surface of a vast ocean and experiencing music, in a kind of hearing that happens on the body, on the skin itself, more pulse than sound maybe. I have no sense of human time.

When I come back to myself I am weeping. A few minutes have passed on the face of the kitchen wall clock. There is release, the sense of a shift in energy. The woman I was, who came into this ordinary apartment, is not the same woman who is leaving.

Perhaps I am experiencing some kind of genetic trace memory, remembering the self as creature of air, as creature of water, as feathered, as finned. The scientists are telling us now (in their guarded way, and with many reservations) that there may be such a thing as genetic memory, trace echoes in the DNA of earlier phases of our history – the eye-blink of the Christian era's scant two millennia, the dream time of our species' journey into self-consciousness, or even the geologic, and I would go so far as to say geomantic, time of our evolution, the script we read in fossils, petrified forests, read in a handful of soil, carried here and there by wayward, unseen rivers. The poetry of the world being itself.

There is something weirdly harmonic in this sense of having lived in another element. All my life, as far back as I can remember, I have dreams where I live in water, can breathe in that element. I wake from these dreams refreshed, as if I've tuned into a part of the self that has yet to know or be distressed by the dualistic and dangerous human sense of being separate from the rest of nature.

Though it goes without saying that the urge to look into the future or the past is as old as the world itself, scrying is the beautiful word we've been using for about five hundred years in English for active clairvoyance: to see images in water, in mirrors, in crystal balls, in bowls filled with ink.

The blank page as scrying medium. I am flying home, thirty-six thousand feet over the Atlantic Ocean, and the blank page of my notebook invites me scry.

II

I go back to the old wells. I start again from scratch. I go back to the first poem that made sense of what instinct was schooling in me.

It's a poem from Gary Snyder's *Regarding Wave*, a collection I first read in or about 1974. At nineteen, I read it as manifesto – though 'manifesto' with its inherent meaning of 'strike with the hand', is, I see now, an inelegant reading of a canny and elegant poem. It's called 'What You Should Know to Be a Poet' and here's how it opens:

all you can about animals as persons.
the names of trees and flowers and weeds.
names of stars, and the movements of the planets
                    and the moon.

your own six senses, with a watchful and elegant mind.

at least one kind of traditional magic:
divination, astrology, the *book of changes*, the tarot;

dreams.
the illusory demons and illusory shining gods;

As I meditate on the poem, line by line, in my sixtieth year to heaven, I see that it has long since become for me a deep well that is constantly refreshed, a source.

This first line, for instance:

all you can about animals as persons.

The Sailor who brings me tea in the morning, brings with the post a new book of poems, *Fur* by Grace Wells, whose name alone grants her entry to this lecture.

Poem after poem deals with the personhood of animals, an ancient, archaic idea that, in the face of so many extinctions in this twenty-first century, makes for an utterance both thrilling and elegiac:

it's not a glimpse of wildness
that I crave, but more like
one of those stories

where the stranger welcomed
into the family home
turns out to be a fox,

or the fisherman's wife
after long years of marriage
proves to be a seal.

['Pace']

There is anger here, too, anger at our temerity in appropriating the creation, and compassion for our pathetically innocent arrogance – so presumptuous of us, this taking upon ourselves the naming of animals.

It reminds me of the urgency of understanding self as animal: the person-hood of the human animal self regained. I resolve to wade out into the inner sea of the self and to ask the dreamgiver to amplify, if it is appropriate, the song whose faint melodic line I intuit out there ahead of me in inchoate space/time.

And that night I dream about the *Voyager* spacecraft and the messages we sent out into space on a gold plated disc in that craft in 1977. I dream the craft is intercepted by another intelligent species. The disc is loaded with information about our blue planet; when these 'aliens' hear familiar music they call a council. What they have heard translates as 'they are killing us'. The song is whale-song. In the dream I can understand it. I even join in. It is a powerful, expressive language, felt on my pulses, a language I understand because I, too, am a native of planet water.

In the way of dreams, next I am helping Seamus Heaney onto a long-boat that has sailed up the mouth of the Liffey – to take him, as he says, 'the old whale roads'. He tells me to make sure that Dublin people know that he appreciated the years of affection (I thought in the dream itself that this was a characteristically apt word), and that his poem, 'Trial Pieces', could be mass produced if there was an emergency and we needed to raise funds. Who are *we*? I wonder when I wake, and I am dogged all morning by these dreams.

I hoke out Heaney's 'Viking Dublin: Trial Pieces' and there I find something very like the twin pulses of my dreams:

> These are trial pieces,
> the craft's mystery
> improvised on bone:
> foliage, bestiaries,
>
> interlacings elaborate
> as the netted route
> of ancestry and trade.
> That have to be
>
> magnified on display
> so that the nostril
> is a migrant prow
> sniffing the Liffey,
>
> swanning it up to the ford,
> dissembling itself
> in antler combs, bone pins,
> coins, weights, scale-pans.

III

Another line from Gary Snyder's poem comes swimming up into my attention then:

> names of stars, and the movements of the planets
> and the moon

To look down at your feet, at the grasses and vetches, at the scribble of the tideline on sand, is one kind of joyous encounter with the world; to look up into the vastness of the heavens prompts another kind of rapture. Profound the meditation on the celestial depths above, their mystery approachable only by the arcane art of pure mathematics or the equally old art of astrology. And the modest human triumph of navigation, the seafarers on our oceans guided by light from stars that are long since dead.

A salute, then, to these nearby companions of Planet Water, the planets of our solar system, who take the bare look off our near sky, whether seen by the naked eye, or by spyglass, telescope, or voyaging space-craft sending home a digitised song of the heavens. These orbiting bodies mythological and actual who trine and sextile, conjunct and square, our natal charts. To know and understand them is to partake of astronomy and astrology both. And of course our moon, visible emblem of the spirit energy named Muse, the usually female enabler of poets and artists. Constant through the ages, if fickle and heartless in the life of an individual artist. 'La Belle Dame Sans Merci', the beautiful woman without mercy – but if you are in her good books, no pun intended, she will guide you to express the sublime heights and depths of the human condition. She of whom Anna Akhmatova has written in 'The Muse':

> When at night I await her coming,
> It seems that life hangs by a strand.
> What are honours, what is youth, what is freedom,
> Compared to that dear guest with rustic pipe in hand

And here is the next line from Snyder that snares my meditating mind:

> your own six senses, with a watchful and elegant mind.

The sixth sense may be the survival sense; the witchy sense, the one that bedrocks vision, hearing, taste, touch, smell. It raises the hackles, it spooks us, it tells us to trust the stranger, to distrust the person known, and vice versa; it sends us messages sometimes through dream, manipulating symbol and event so that we say, I feel it in my bones, I feel it in my waters. The sixth sense may also be common sense, available to all, though sometimes it feels like the rarest of human attributes.

And observing these senses, with a watchful and elegant mind? Watchful mind: like a hunter who must recognise tracks and trails and scat patterns, a voyager who reads current and wind patterns, who recognises and interprets with all the senses engaged. Elegant mind: mind shaped by human practice but aware of animal self – this is how I have come to think of this part of Snyder's injunction, or advice, or suggestion, or imperative, his *ars poetica*.

The etymology of elegant contains the notion of choice from the Latin *legere*. It is related, again through the Latin, to the word elect. So elegance is a schooled grace, a chosen arrangement of elements.

And I am led on, elegantly, to:

> at least one kind of traditional magic:
> divination, astrology, the *book of changes*, the tarot;

I have my old *I Ching* to hand – *The Book of Changes* rendered into English by Cary F. Baynes from the Richard Wilhelm translation into German from the Chinese original, with a foreword by Carl Gustav Jung – a piece of flotsam from the zeitgeist tide of my youth. Though the self now would critique the translation, and critique the living of one's life by the throw of yarrow sticks or coins, the space that the engagement with the book opens is still a space I value. The watchful mind – this time allowing itself take time out to watch the patterns that the energies of the life are mirroring back. Divination is a kind of mirroring, reading the self through external symbols or systems of symbolic coding. Not too different to reading a poem.

The *I Ching*, so often consulted – but only once used to determine an actual decision.

Back in 1978 I lived for some months on a small island, Papa Stour, in the Shetland Islands halfway from here to Iceland, in a small croft within yards of the sea. In the calm of the solstice, the bay below the house was a saucer of blue milk but there were also nights when the waves battered at the door. Literally battered at the door. There was candle light and a cranky range that I beachcombed to feed in order to heat water and to cook.

I was fit and strong and slept in the song of the sea, rocked in dreams that made me write in a fluid emotionally free way as the moods and the humours washed through me. Learning the names of the flowers and birds and fishes and creatures, and walking beyond the dyke where the ruined watermills are.

I spent long stretches alone in a kind of rapture. Papa Stour supports a large colony of arctic terns, a significant presence of arctic skuas and ringed plover. There are populations of fulmar, shag, guillemot, black guillemot, razorbill, great black-backed gull and kittiwake. Learning their names was an excitement. The geomorphology was an excitement: to walk in beauty, in an internal rhapsody, the iteration and reiteration of patterning in cliffs, stacks, geos, caves, blowholes, storm beaches and wave-lashed bedrock.

There, too, the detritus of western civilisation colourfully pooling in coves. Plastics. Blue bleach bottles, green toilet ducks, plastic bags riding the currents like jellyfish, plastic fish-boxes, the odd boat fender and other items of good honest pruck, an oar, a well-made box, old glass floats, occasionally a beautiful piece of sculpture made by the sea herself.

I nearly didn't write poetry at all, it seemed like such a puny act compared to the forces of nature shaping and energising this place.

There could be no competition in craft terms. Could I harness some of this power? Was there a lesson in it for my poetry?

I call up, to give myself courage, some words from a poem by my old craft teacher, the poet James McAuley, which contains the nub of what I wanted from my relationship with the world as it was opening to me as a young woman:

> I learn again to take pains
> With simple things: to take
> The knife in my better hand, so;
> And the driftwood, already worn
> By the steely waves to a shape
> I recognize as if dreamt
> While I rocked in those waves myself—
> The wood in this hand, so.
>
> The mask of one I recognize
> Stares up from the wood. I begin.

['Ritual']

I felt full of airy lightness. I persisted with the notebooks. And then one morning I wrote some lines that I read with sudden understanding – I scanned what I had written with a cold eye, the eye of another gaze as it were. I knew then that I would publish what I was writing. I was writing then for someone who was other than myself to read. Whoever that reader was, I was grateful she came at that moment. That flash of understanding was the intimation of the journey I would make again and again, the journey I still make, or aspire to making, again and again: the critical distance. The journey from a purely expressive mode to something I was beginning to understand as art.

But on the island of Papa Stour the autumn was coming in – soon it would be the equinox. Look, the crofters would say, do you see any trees?

Even the mice have curly tails to cling on in the winter winds. I loved that scoured landscape but I began to fear the prospect of a long dark winter alone. I had enough money to buy in fuel for the winter, for beachcombing would get more and more difficult, or to buy a ticket to return to Dublin.

One night, by firelight, I threw the yarrow sticks in the order the *I Ching* asks for and while completing the somewhat laborious ritual I opened my mind to the question: would I go home to Dublin?

I got the hexagram Fu – Return. One of the lines in the hexagram was a moving line with the interpretation – Noblehearted return. No remorse. Which seven years later I rendered into the title of my first collection of poems, *Return and No Blame*.

If I throw the *I Ching* now it is usually to slow the world down a bit, that I might connect to an old and well-loved book in whose pages there still nestles a dried thrift, *armeria maritima*, a wild flower from those days in the lull of the tides.

Opening the book of changes brings memory of closing the door of 'The Mellings', that croft on the lip of the bay; it is to recall that autumn morning when I hitched a ride in a nifty little ketch across the Sound of Papa, and went on to Lerwick of the fine fiddle playing, to Aberdeen of the witch-burners, to Stranraer, and across to Larne where they took me in and interrogated me – always a problem for the young, explaining a feckless existence to the authorities. I told them the lyrics in my books were for songs, watching them paw suspiciously through my salt-stained notebooks.

Back home to the deep filthy breath of the river, back to the turf-smoke of north inner city Dublin, the smell of my childhood, to a decrepit room on the elegant Georgian crescent of Beresford Place, on the banks of the river I have loved above all rivers, the river Eavan Boland evokes and embodies in her masterwork 'Anna Liffey':

In the end
It will not matter
That I was a woman. I am sure of it.
The body is a source. Nothing more.
There is a time for it. There is a certainty
About the way it seeks its own dissolution.
Consider rivers.
They are always en route to
Their own nothingness. From the first moment
They are going home. And so
When language cannot do it for us,
Cannot make us know love will not diminish us,
There are these phrases
Of the ocean
To console us.
Particular and unafraid of their completion.
In the end
Everything that burdened and distinguished me
Will be lost in this:
I was a voice.

IV

This time of year, the shortening days of November, I like to go walking
the estuary of a morning, to observe the newly arrived Brent geese.
They look thin and exhausted after their three and a half thousand
mile trip. They leave eastern High Arctic Canada where they hatch
and raise their young, they stage in Greenland and in western Iceland
and they over-winter with us in north-west Europe, chiefly here in
Ireland but also in western Britain and northern France. They'll be
my winter music in the sky above my head as they commute from the
estuary to the sports fields behind our house, fattening, fattening. I
am always relieved to see the geese back: something in the greater
cycles is working.

In last night's dream I was part of a flock of Brent, bearing down on Ireland. I was cruising in the wake of the leading bird, knowing in my goose brain that I was heading for Strangford Lough. I felt very happy as part of the flock, enjoying the tension of wind in my feathers, the bird's eye view of the beautiful Antrim coastline.

I'm sure the dream was influenced by my journeys on Google Earth the night before, for I had been cruising around over the Shetland Islands, bringing back into mind the croft on the edge of the bay, so liberating in its way, this virtual, digitised flying.

My own Sailor made the journey from Iceland to Dublin late this summer, traditionally a time to catch good winds. But not this trip. A journey that was expected to take eight days turned into an eighteen-day struggle, first storm-bound in the Westmann Islands, then beating for days into opposing seas. For much of this time I was out of contact with The Sailor, I had no idea of how they were faring, him and his shipmates. I didn't like one bit the look of what I could pull down online from the weather sites.

A friend from a fishing family in Howth tells me her mother called the opening to the harbour the Gates of Hell. Better, the sea-wives of old believed, not to know what is happening out there when there is nothing to be done about it. I go into a semi-atavistic state when The Sailor is on the sea: candles and jujus and lucky stones. The world is always laden with, drenched in, portent.

I have only myself to blame that The Sailor *is* a sailor. It was, after all, at my prompting that he first began to voyage out on the deep. When we first met he didn't sail. I'd known his poetry before I met him and assumed he was a sailor, for the imagery, the metaphors, the diction is all of the sea and the craft of sailing, as in, to take an example at random, 'The Sea Gypsy and Her Lover', this passage that now, after all his subsequent long journeys under sail, has a hauntedness it never had when he wrote it:

Turning and building back always on my heart
I am the oldest port you ever sailed for,
Mine in the dog-watch is the unseen hand
That pulls the helm over into the belly of a wave,
Mine and mine only the brief skyward path
Climbing the silver inside of the uproll when the moon spins
And the heart screams inward home, home —

I am the music then,
I am the clash of bracelets and the space hung
Where the seabird was,
Mindless and cold like the murmuring of the surf,
Nailed for all time to the crossmast of your bones.

After his first long crossing, a journey from Antigua in the Caribbean to
Kinsale in his home county of Cork, I stood in the star fort that overlooks
the entry to Kinsale harbour and watched the speck far out on the ocean
gradually become the seventy-footer it actually was as it swept elegantly
past. When he stepped ashore I asked him what it was like out there. 'A
vaaaast ocean. Why do we call our world Planet Earth?'

When the signs and portents on his latest voyage got too much for me,
him out of touch and out of reach, out there beyond the gates of hell –
I called myself back to my senses with a neatly made nine-liner, 'A
Postcard from Iceland' by Seamus Heaney; it was for me a reassuring
handclasp, a steadier from that steady man:

As I dipped to test the stream some yards away
From a hot spring, I could hear nothing
But the whole mud-slick muttering and boiling.

And then my guide behind me saying,
'Lukewarm. And I think you'd want to know
That *luk* was an old Icelandic word for hand.'

And you would want to know (but you know already)
How usual that waft and pressure felt
When the inner palm of water found my palm.

V

Sometimes, as now, when immersed in some task of writing, the tides wash in something apposite to one's purpose. As, today, from another book in the post, this: a patient, Kathleen, presents to Doctor Jim Lucey at St Patrick's University Hospital, Dublin. I quote Doctor Lucey:

> One day I was sitting in the special care unit listening to a woman whose thoughts and behaviour were very disorganized by a manic psychosis. Her story appeared to be going nowhere, and so after a while, we agreed to end our conversation. Despite her distraction, she was thankful for our meeting. As she went to the door, she turned back and said: 'By the way, doctor, did I ever tell you that my mother was a fish?'

The claim is startling to her doctor and to his readers, precisely because we are aware that the woman is very unwell and that the statement is made in a therapeutic environment.

That utterance in a poetry workshop, on the other hand, if presented as a line in a poem, would not be considered odd. We might put the line under pressure to see if it worked in the context of the other lines around it:

'My mother was a fish/ but my father was a dragon'
'My mother was a fish, a cold fish'
'My mother was a fish who/ floundered on the shore'
'My mother was a fish/ and had a finny spine'
'My mother was a fish, Pisces/my father was a centaur, Sagittarius'

I might direct the workshop participant to Nuala Ní Dhomhnaill's beautiful poem 'A Recovered Memory of Water' in its translation from the original Irish by Paul Muldoon:

[71]

Sometimes when the mermaid's daughter
is in the bathroom
cleaning her teeth with a thick brush
and baking soda
she has the sense the room is filling
with water.

It starts at her feet and ankles
and slides further and further up
over her thighs and hips and waist.

Or I might recall lines from Adrienne Rich's 'Diving into the Wreck', her game altering classic of the American tradition:

First the air is blue and then
it is bluer and then green and then
black I am blacking out and yet
my mask is powerful
it pumps my blood with power
the sea is another story
the sea is not a question of power
I have to learn alone
to turn my body without force
in the deep element.

Or I might give the workshop no direction. I might ask the other participants what they would do if it was their own line, their own poem, as if what they were reading was an early draft of a poem put away until now – it's a technique I've picked up from projective dreamwork practice, useful for thwarting the unhelpful cleverality of the red biro merchants who are all too quick to jump in with: 'what's wrong with this poem is ...'

Whatever has brought the workshop participant to the phrase 'My mother was a fish', by the time it is shared, by the time it is uttered in the poetry workshop, it is treated simply as a line of poetry.

The poetry workshop can for sure be a healing place, as it can be a wounding place. But, and we do well to remember this, it is not a psychiatrist's treatment room. I like to think it has the smell of cedar oil, of wood shavings or welding, of the sweat that goes into the well-made craft to carry us the journey we have to make.

Or perhaps it has that indefinable salty smell of a capable boat that is fit for its journey, a boat like the one that did, in the end, bring The Sailor home again.

VI

What was I doing, I ask myself, when he was out there on the trackless wastes, if not scrying? And so I am back again to Snyder and his advocacy of 'some kind of traditional magic'. Which, walking the beach at Balscadden and gazing hopefully out to sea, brought to mind Yeats and his faith in the tarot. The Elemental Tarot (published in 1988), a relatively young deck, the tarot deck I use myself, takes the four elements as the organising principle. Where traditional tarot decks would use Cups, this deck has Water. Where Coins or Pentacles, this deck has Earth, where Wands Fire, where Swords Air. The major arcana of the traditional deck become the Spirit cards of the Elemental Tarot.

The Elemental Tarot draws on many cultures for its symbols, from religion, mythology, astrology, numerology, philosophy. Reading a card, reading a spread of cards, is a looking into the self, into the mirror, in the same way reading a poem is a looking into the self. It is also a looking at the limit of selfhood. The poem is reading you as the spread is reading you, reading where you come from, what you bring to it, your education, your tolerance, your ear, your heartbeat, your experience, your insight, your vocabulary, your history, and your understanding of your history.

It allows an unlocking of the door between the subconscious and the quotidian.

Once in County Leitrim, deep in lake and river country, I laid a spread, the ten card Celtic Cross Spread using the Elemental Tarot, to break through a writing block. It was November, a winter at the end of the eighties. I wrote a short poem for each of the cards, just letting whatever floated to mind and ear form the line. They were the last poems written in that house. And that winter was the last winter of my marriage. With hindsight, I could say the cards and poems made a narrative that 'foretold' what would happen. But I couldn't see that then. All I wanted were the poems. I called the ten-poem sequence 'Mysteries of the Home'.

One of them, the first card drawn for the spread, The Querent, who stands for the one who is seeking, gave me this poem, 'Well':

> I know this path by magic not by sight.
> Behind me on the hillside the cottage light
> is like a star that's gone astray. The moon
> is waning fast, each blade of grass a rune
> inscribed by hoarfrost. This path's well worn.
> I lug a bucket by bramble and blossoming blackthorn.
> I know this path by magic not by sight.
> Next morning when I come home quite unkempt
> I cannot tell what happened at the well.
> You spurn my explanation of a sex spell
> cast by the spirit who guards the source
> that boils deep in the belly of the earth,
> even when I show you what lies strewn
> in my bucket – a golden waning moon,
> seven silver stars, our own porch light,
> your face at the window staring into the dark.

And that started the cycle of prediction. One day soon after, soldiers were on the road with a megaphone warning us not to drink the water from the taps. It was coming straight from the River Shannon, and, as there had been a fire at the utility plant that normally treated the water, now our water was untreated and toxic. That the water could be so dangerous, this close to the source of the Shannon, was an unsettling notion. There was a flurry of activity around the old wells, cleaning them out and fixing them up, all to find potable water – and suddenly there I was, in my thirties, going to the well for water.

I recite the poem now as a spell against the frackers, the energy companies who want to extract the natural gas from the carboniferous shale that underlies the whole of our beautiful lake district, Fermanagh and Leitrim, under the land and under the lakes where our bounteous aquifers are. The fracking process risks poisoning the wells: it will be impossible to prevent the toxic residues from entering the water table, from polluting the aquifers. The rivers don't recognise the border, the lakes do not recognise the border, the underground aquifers for sure don't recognise the border.

Have I water on the brain? I have a vaaaaast ocean between my ears. I fear for my blood pressure, for the frail pump that keeps fluid circulating in my arterial system, I fear that any minute now I shall get on to the subject of 'Shell to Sea' or Irish Water. I lift a shell from my bookshelf and the lull of tides is mine for the hearing.

VII

I let the Library Angel direct my hand along the bookshelf and it comes to rest at the *Tao Te Ching*. Or, as it is variously known, *The Book of the Immanence of the Way*, *The Book of the Way and How It Manifests Itself in the World*, or *The Book of the Way*. Written down sometime in the fifth century BCE by the archivist Laotzu, though we are not even certain if *this* is fact, it is full of simple, clear, shining wisdom. Stephen Mitchell, poet and translator (notably of Rilke), remarks in the introduction: 'If I haven't always translated Laotzu's words, my intention has always been to translate his mind.'

I open the book at random and find this:

> The supreme good is like water,
> which nourishes all things without trying to.
> It is content with the low places that people disdain.

And then this:

> The Tao is always at ease.
> It overcomes without competing,
> answers without speaking a word,
> arrives without being summoned,
> accomplishes without a plan.
>
> Its net covers the whole universe.
> And though its meshes are wide,
> it doesn't let a thing slip through.

This calms me down. Enough to tackle the last part of the opening, just the opening section mind, of Snyder's poem, 'What You Should Know to Be a Poet' – that early source whose promptings I have been following through this lecture:

> dreams.
> the illusory demons and illusory shining gods;

I started an early apprenticeship to my maternal grandmother Mary McCarthy as a dreamer, a reader of dreams, a facility which segued easily, smoothly, into reading poetry. Mary's dreams were so vivid I can remember them across fifty years, and the adult sees what the child could not: how they were used to manage her daughters. I would be under the table listening to the images – violent, bloody, apocalyptic, dramatic. Sometimes genuinely prophetic: I witnessed a number of dreams where she had one of her emigrant children manifest on the dream plane, a vision of the son or daughter, or some sign of them. She would start to clean like a demon, all vim and vigour, and sure enough there would come the longed-for knock at the door.

At other times the dream would presage the other kind of knock. The bad news knock. The telegram from overseas.

This calling from the void of colour, of excitement, of a virtual theatrical space where anything, anything, might happen left the child I was spellbound. I was plumbing the mysterious depths of the imagination, the image-making faculty within which is so close to the poetic act, a kind of wide-awake dreaming in the language, in the moment. Sometimes delighted; sometimes terrified.

Later, much later, I would go on to learn about dreamworking, about projective dreamwork, and learn how we dream for our communities, how we dream for each other.

From my other grandmother, Hannah, I keep a dog-eared Italian oleograph of the kind that were once commonplace in prayer books. It is Stella Maris, Our Lady Star of the Sea. The hymn I learned at Hannah's knee goes with the image, is, in effect, the tune to look at the image to:

> Hail, Queen of Heaven, the Ocean Star,
> Guide of the wanderer here below,
> Thrown on life's surge, we claim thy care,
> Save us from peril and from woe.
> Mother of Christ, Star of the sea
> Pray for the wanderer, pray for me.

In robes of star-spangled blue she stands on a crescent moon, a star on her brow.

VIII
Pat Boran in his poem 'The Shape of Water' speaks of

> great telescopes and simple mirrors
> water leaves for us everywhere
> to show the connections between things,
> to show us what we really are.

Water pooling, reflecting, refracting light, his poem reminds us we are ourselves seventy per cent water, that the planet is seventy-five per cent water, that four days without it and we'd be on the threshold of death. He conjures up the famous Apollo images of the Earth seen from space:

> Blue planet the astronauts brought
> home to grey cities and green fields;
> blue eye of the quest for knowledge
> turning in the heavens; blue, blue,
> the planet Earth, which is really the planet Water,
> a raindrop in the light of distant stars.

Holy, holy, holy water: I remember the font inside the front door in 22E Upper Sean McDermott Street, molded glass of a blue hue with an inset cross in mother of pearl, a little shrine to water, always a blessing leaving home in my prelapsarian innocence.

I remember walking one Christmas with my father across the river to the well and shrine of Saint Albert in the Carmelite Church in Whitefriar Street. An old neighbour of ours, bent double, literally, the village crone of the fairytales, who scared the wits out of me, believed the water had a cure for arthritis. Saint Albert's Holy Water: the word holy itself, of course, remembers an older meaning of *whole, healthy*. Not that my father believed in the Sicilian Saint Albert, but he believed in our old neighbour.

I see my father before me in his own mystery, walking down Gardiner Street to the river. He chivvies me along, and soon he'll raise me on his shoulders, to make time in the dark. I'll see over the bridge's parapet the lights on the flowing river.

IX

From the amniotic fluid, the protective waters of our pre-birth dreamtime, to the very last sip, all water is holy water. The blessing to the living and the dying is rendered here by Carol Ann Duffy, from her elegy for her mother, May Black from County Carlow, in a poetry that irrigates the spirit in a hard time:

Water. The times I'd call as a child
for a drink, till you'd come, sit on the edge
of the bed in the dark, holding my hand,
just as we held hands now and you died.

A good last word.
                    Nights since I've cried, but gone
to my own child's side with a drink, watched
her gulp it down then sleep. *Water.*
What a mother brings
                    through darkness still
to her parched daughter.

I raise a glass of clear water to all my comrades in this work of ours; I point my craft out to sea and trust to the winds that have brought me this far, borne up on mystery; I take my leave with the words of John Montague singing in my ear:

For there is no sea
it is all a dream
there is no sea
except in the tangle
of our minds:
the wine dark
sea of history
on which we all turn
turn and thresh
    and disappear.
                      [From Section IV 'Wine Dark Sea' of 'Sea Changes']

A transcript of a lecture given in University College Dublin, on 26 November 2016.
For Rachael Hegarty

BIOGRAPHICAL NOTE

PAULA MEEHAN was born in Dublin and educated at Trinity College Dublin and at Eastern Washington University. She has published six original award winning collections of poetry: *Return and No Blame* (1984), *Reading the Sky* (1986), *The Man Who Was Marked by Winter* (1991), *Pillow Talk* (1994), *Dharmakaya* (2000) and *Painting Rain* (2009). *Geomantic* is forthcoming in November of 2016 from Dedalus Press, Dublin. She has also written plays for adults and children and has held residencies in universities, in prisons and in the wider community. She has received the Butler Literary Award for Poetry, presented by the Irish American Cultural Institute, the Marten Toonder Award for Literature, the Denis Devlin Award (for *Dharmakaya*), and the PPI Award for Radio Drama. In 2015 she received the Lawrence O'Shaughnessy Award for Irish Poetry and was inducted into the Hennessy Literary Hall of Fame. Meehan is a member of Aosdána and was Ireland Professor of Poetry from 2013 to 2016.

ACKNOWLEDGEMENTS

My thanks to Noelle Moran and Damien Lynam of UCD Press who shepherded this book into being.

I wish to acknowledge with deep gratitude the support of the members of the Ireland Chair of Poetry Trust – Ciaran Carson, Mary Clayton, Bob Collins, Sir Donnell Deeny, QC, Nicholas Grene, Adrian Hall, Michael Longley, CBE, Sheila Pratschke and Brian Walker. My particular thanks to the Trust's administrator, Niamh McCabe. Their many kindnesses and dedication have made possible the work I did during the three years, 2013 to 2016, when I was Ireland Professor of Poetry.

My thanks to the students, the poets, and the scholars of the three universities, who offered me sustaining friendship and engagement. My thanks to the many interested parties in and out of the colleges who joined in the conversation in schools, in community centres, in libraries, in workshops, in the streets.

My thanks to Kate and Joan Newmann for hospitality and support in facilitating community outreach from Queen's University, Belfast; to Michael Egan for facilitating work with R.A.D.E, my main outreach project from Trinity College Dublin; to Ursula Byrne, Head of Development and Strategic Programmes, for facilitating an archive project at the James Joyce Library in University College Dublin.

Mindful that I took up this position a fortnight after the death of Seamus Heaney, our beloved Nobel Laureate, in whose name the Trust was founded, and mindful of how committed and enthusiastic a member of the Trust he was, I wish to thank Marie Heaney for her support and goodwill in such a time of sorrow.

And finally, my love and thanks to Theo Dorgan, with me every step of the journey.

The author and publisher gratefully acknowledge the following for permission to reprint copyright material. Every effort has been made to seek copyright clearance on referenced text. If there are any omissions, UCD Press will be pleased to insert the appropriate acknowledgement in any subsequent printing or editions.

Anna Akhmatova: excerpt from 'The Muse', from *The Complete Poems of Anna Akhmatova*, translated by Judith Hemschemeyer, edited and introduced by Roberta Reeder. Copyright © 1989, 1992, 1997 by Judith Hemschemeyer. Reprinted with the permission of The Permissions Company, Inc., on behalf of Zephyr Press, www.zephyrpress.org.

'Sestina' from POEMS by Elizabeth Bishop. Copyright © 2011 by The Alice H. Methfessel Trust. Publisher's Note and compilation copyright © 2011 by Farrar, Straus and Giroux, LLC. Reprinted by kind permission of Farrar, Straus and Giroux, LLC.

Eavan Boland: 'Amber', from *Domestic Violence* (Carcanet, 2007). Reprinted by kind permission of Carcanet Press.

Sandy Denny: excerpt from 'Who Knows Where the Time Goes'. Published for the World ex USA & Canada by Fairwood Music (UK) Ltd Copyright © 1968 the Estate of Sandy Denny. All Rights Reserved. International Copyright Secured. Reprinted by kind permission of Elizabeth Hurtt and Fairwood Music.

Nuala Ní Dhomhnaill: excerpt from 'A Recovered Memory of Water', from *The Fifty Minute Mermaid*, poems in Irish by Nuala Ní Dhomhnaill, translated by Paul Muldoon (The Gallery Press, 2007). Reprinted by kind permission of The Gallery Press.

Theo Dorgan: excerpt from 'The Sea Gypsy and her Lover', from *The Ordinary House of Love* (Salmon Poetry, 1991, reprinted by Dedalus Press, 2008). Reprinted by kind permission of Dedalus Press.

BIBLIOGRAPHY

Anna Akhmatova: 'The Muse', from *The Complete Poems of Anna Akhmatova*, translated by Judith Hemschemeyer, edited and introduced by Roberta Reeder (Zephyr Press, 1989).

W. H. Auden: 'Musée des Beaux Arts', from *Collected Poems* (Faber and Faber, 1976).

Elizabeth Bishop: 'Sestina', from *Poems* (Farrar, Straus and Giroux, 2011).

Eavan Boland: 'Amber', from *Domestic Violence* (Carcanet, 2007) and 'Anna Liffey', from *In a Time of Violence* (Carcanet Press, 1994).

Pat Boran: 'The Shape of Water', from *The Shape of Water* (Dedelus Press, 1996).

C. P. Cavafy: 'When They Come Alive', from *Selected Poems*, translated by Avi Sharon (Penguin, 2008).

Thomas Charles-Edwards and Fergus Kelly, edited by: *Bechbretha/Bee Judgements* (Dublin Institute of Advanced Studies, 1983).

Sandy Denny: 'Who Knows Where the Time Goes' (Fairwood Music, 1968).

Nuala Ní Dhomhnaill: 'A Recovered Memory of Water', from *The Fifty Minute Mermaid*, poems in Irish by Nuala Ní Dhomhnaill, translated by Paul Muldoon (The Gallery Press, 2007).

Emily Dickinson: 'I Died for Beauty but Was Scarce', from *The Selected Poems*, edited by Conrad Aiken (The Modern Library, 1924).

Theo Dorgan: 'The Sea Gypsy and her Lover', from *The Ordinary House of Love* (Salmon Poetry, 1991, reprinted by Dedalus Press, 2008).

Carol Ann Duffy: 'Bees' and 'Water', from *The Bees* (Picador, 2011).

Seamus Heaney: 'A Postcard from Iceland', from *The Haw Lantern* (Faber and Faber, 1987) and 'Viking Dublin: Trial Pieces', from *North* (Faber and Faber, 1975).

Jim Holland: 'The Romance of Bees', *The Irish Beekeeper* (November, 2013).

Galway Kinnell: 'The Bear', from *Three Books* (Houghton Mifflin Harcourt, 1993).

Joanne Kyger: 'Destruction', from *Collected Poems: About Now* (National Poetry Foundation, 2007).

Lao-tzu: *Tao Te Ching: A New English Version,* translated by Stephen Mitchell (Harper Collins, 1988).

Louis MacNeice: 'The Island', from *Ten Burnt Offerings* (Faber and Faber, 1951).

James J. McAuley: 'Ritual', from *New and Selected Poems* (Dedalus Press, 2005).

Paula Meehan: 'The Solace of Artemis' is included from *20|12: Twenty Irish Poets Respond to Science in Twelve Lines,* edited by Iggy McGovern (Dedalus Press *cum* Quaternia Press 2012); 'The Old Professor', from *Geomantic,* (Dedalus Press, 2016) and 'Well', from the sequence 'Mysteries of the Home' reprinted in *Mysteries of the Home* (Dedalus Press, 2013).

John Montague: 'Wine Dark Sea', from the sequence 'Sea Changes' in *Tides* (The Gallery Press, 1971).

Marianne Moore: 'Poetry', from *Observations* (The Dial Press, 1924) and 'Poetry', from *The Complete Poems of Marianne Moore* (The Macmillan Company/ The Viking Press, 1967), and 'Ten Answers: Letters from an October Afternoon, Part II', *Harper's Magazine,* 229 (November 1964).

Kate Newmann: 'Pasiphae Sat, Old and in Black', from *The Blind Woman in the Blue House* (Summer Palace Press, 2001).

Adrienne Rich: 'Diving into the Wreck', from *Diving into the Wreck: Poems 1971–72* (W. W. Norton and Co., 1973).

Theodore Roethke: 'Third Meditation', from *Words for the Wind* (Secker and Warburg, 1957).

Gary Snyder: 'What You Should Know to Be a Poet', from *Regarding Wave* (New Directions, 1970).

Colm Tóibín: *The Testament of Mary* (Scribner's, 2012).

Grace Wells: 'Pace', from *Fur* (Dedalus Press, 2015).

W. B. Yeats: excerpt from *Autobiographies* (Macmillan and Company, 1955).